Old Kintyre
by Carol McNeill

The burn at Waterfoot was often used by Carradale's fishermen to moor their boats in winter, as Carradale pier did not provide an all-weather harbour for boats and in certain winds, such as north-easterlies, boats were unable to lie there and steamers were unable to land. As this photograph was probably taken in summertime, these boats were probably 'cleaning' before the opening of the herring season. A very picturesque spot, Waterfoot has inspired many artists and in the 1930s was the centre of an artistic community with a studio at the water's edge.

© Carol McNeill, 2007.
First published in the United Kingdom, 2007,
by Stenlake Publishing Ltd.
www.stenlake.co.uk
ISBN 9781840333992

The coal smack *Euphemia* of Carradale, which carried up to 32 tons of coal between Troon and Campbeltown for more than twenty years, pictured at Port Righ bay around 1912. Built in Ardrossan in the late nineteenth century, she was owned and worked by Gilbert and James MacIntosh. The man wearing the bowler hat is almost certainly Matthew MacDougall, the Port Righ boat-builder. He built several fine skiffs in the early 1900s, helped by his fishermen sons in the off-season, using pitch pine from Clydesdale and larch trees from Saddell. He built his boats in a field near the family home and part of the roadside dyke had to be removed before a skiff could be manhandled with ropes, rollers and the help of local fishermen into the bay.

Further Reading

The books listed below were used by the author during her research. None of them is available from Stenlake Publishing. Those interested in finding out more are advised to contact their local bookshop or reference library.

Argyllshire Herald archives
Campbeltown Courier archives
Campbeltown, Southend and Machrihanish Guide (1907)
The Campbeltown Book, Kintyre Civic Society (2003)
The Kintyre Antiquarian and Natural History Magazine
Skipness: Memories of a Highland Estate, Angus Graham (2005)
The Ring-Net Fishermen, Angus Martin (1981)
Kintyre, The Hidden Past, Angus Martin (1984)
Kintyre Country Life, Angus Martin (2005)
Tarbert Past and Present, Dugald Mitchell (1886, reprinted 1996)
Kintyre, Norman Newton (1999)
The Story of Gigha, the Flourishing Island, Kathleen Philip (1979)

Acknowledgements

This book could never have been written without the help, information and patient co-operation from a number of local people. In particular, I would like to thank Angus Martin who once again shared his encyclopedic knowledge of local history so freely and with no regard for the time it took from his own writing. Many thanks are also due to Maureen Bell, Moira Burgess, Shelagh Cameron, Frances Hood, Olive Lees, Ian MacDonald, Ian Y. Macintyre, Elizabeth Marrison, Jim and Margaret Miller, Fiona Sellers, and Elaine and Jeremy Wright. I would like to dedicate this book to the memory of my father and mother, John and Nancy Burgess, without whom I would never have known the delights of being brought up in the Kintyre peninsula.

The publishers wish to thank the following for contributing photographs to this book: Emslie and Ian MacPherson for the inside front and back covers and pages 1, 2, 5, 8, 17-19, 25, 26 (upper), 27 (both), 28, 29, 31-34, 36, 37, 39, 40 (upper), 41-45 and 48; Maureen Bell for pages 26 (lower), 30, 40 (lower), 46 and the back cover; Cnoc Araich Publishing for page 38; and the author for pages 13, 14 and 24.

INTRODUCTION

Only the narrow neck of land less than a mile wide between East and West Loch Tarbert keeps the peninsula of Kintyre part of the Scottish mainland. Indeed, as every Kintyre schoolchild knows - or at least used to be taught - King Magnus of Norway claimed it in 1098 by keeping to the letter of the law spelt out in a treaty between Scotland and Norway which gave him the right to 'all the islands off the west coasts which were separated by water navigable by a ship with rudder set.' The story goes that he sat in his galley and held on to the tiller while he was pulled across the isthmus from east to west. It was a cunning move by someone who has come down in history with the slightly derisory name of Magnus Barelegs, thanks to the knee-length tunic of the area which he claimed.

For such a relatively small piece of land - about 40 miles long and between six and eight miles across - Kintyre encompasses an amazing range of scenery, from lush flat pastureland to hills and waterfalls, with the breath-taking Atlantic waves on the west coast crashing on golden sands, complemented by the quieter Firth of Clyde on the east. Kintyre also provides a haven for many rare species of wildlife and several areas have been designated by Scottish Natural Heritage as Sites of Special Scientific Interest.

Kintyre is home to a wealth of ancient history and archaeology, with links to Somerled, Lord of the Isles, and Robert the Bruce. Traces of early inhabitants can still be found, with examples of Iron Age forts and duns, Bronze Age burial cairns, standing stones, cup-and-ring markings, and Neolithic cists scattered over the length and breadth of the peninsula. As well as the impressive Saddell Abbey, remains of mediaeval Christian chapels can be seen at Southend, Kilchousland near Peninver, Kilkivan and Kilkenzie, and also off-shore on the nearby islands of Sanda and Gigha. Old grave slabs commemorating mediaeval soldiers and clerics, as well as those engaged in more down-to-earth activities such as farming or seafaring, can still be seen in various degrees of preservation. An enormous debt of gratitude is owed to the Kintyre Antiquarian and Natural History Society which over the years has recorded and preserved so many of these ancient landmarks.

The two main towns, Campbeltown and Tarbert, feature on all the milestones as marker points on the peninsula. The main A83 road on the west coast links the two, with the B842 scenic route cutting across from Kennacraig, outside Tarbert, to Claonaig and then down the east coast through Carradale to Campbeltown. Southend also has an alternative route to Campbeltown, the Leerside Road, as well as eight miles of single-track road twisting tortuously down to the Mull of Kintyre itself. Before the use of explosives to blast rock, the old 'post road' taken by the Campbeltown to Tarbert mail coach was the high road through Kintyre. That route left the present A83 at Drum, near Kilkenzie, and followed on to Tangy village, Killocraw and Putechan, before coming back down to shore level at High Bellochantuy. Villages such as Muasdale, Tayinloan and Whitehouse were regular stopping points for passengers and cargo, as well as the Royal Mail.

Where transport is concerned, it could be said that it might be easier to get to and from Kintyre if it were an actual island, as the once-regular steamers have long been discontinued, leaving the long road to Glasgow as the main means of travel, with the alternative of flying from Machrihanish Airport. There has never been a national rail network in Kintyre, although the narrow gauge Campbeltown & Machrihanish Light Railway was a popular service between 1906 and 1932.

Kintyre is quite possibly the first part of Scotland where the Gaelic language was spoken. Native Gaelic has now sadly died out on the peninsula, with Muasdale on the west coast the last village to retain it. Gaelic was seen as somehow inferior to English and was actively discouraged. One former pupil at Cleit school in the early 1920s still remembers being caned for speaking Gaelic which was considered a 'useless language' at the time. His parents were both native Gaelic speakers, but latterly the older generation only spoke in their mother tongue so that their children or outsiders would be unable to understand what they were saying. The author's late mother-in-law, born in Campbeltown in 1898, would occasionally come out with a Gaelic word or phrase, but when asked for the meaning would brush it aside in near-embarrassment.

The language lives on in many place names, including Ronachan ('place of seals'), Tayinloan ('marsh house') and Ben Gullion ('hill of shoulders') - and Kintyre itself comes from the Gaelic *Cinntire*, meaning the 'head of the land' or 'land's end'. Other place names are of Norse origin from the early invaders - Saddell ('sandy valley'), Skipness ('ship point'), Muasdale ('valley of the monks'), and Tangy ('tongue of land') are just some of these.

As with many other parts of Scotland, one of Kintyre's main exports was its people, who travelled to America, Canada and Australia in search of a better livelihood for themselves and their families. They often named their new settlements after towns, villages or districts in the 'old country', and today echoes of Kintyre place names can be found in Queensland (Kilkivan Shire), New South Wales (Campbelltown) and Ontario (Tayinloan, Killean, Largie and Barrhill). More than 400 people in the parish of Killean and Kilkenzie alone emigrated in 1840. In what became known as the 'six wet years' from around 1839, when the potato and oats crops failed in the constant rainfall, people began to starve as their staple diet disappeared. Large numbers went to Australia or New Zealand - a journey which in the 1830s took four months by sea from Oban. Ontario was chosen by many farmers to relocate to, as its land was in many ways similar to that which they had left behind; but no matter how skilled they were with animals or crops, they were designated only as 'agricultural labourers' in the records of their adopted countries.

With the once all-essential fishing industry diminished beyond recognition, and other industries struggling to survive, Kintyre has a high rate of unemployment which has never been helped by the sense of comparative remoteness from the central belt. However, recent initiatives to encourage visitors to come to discover for themselves Kintyre's scenic beauty and heritage are encouraging, and surely this is a part of Scotland which is well worth visiting and to keep coming back to.

Tarbert, with its commanding position at the head of the Kintyre peninsula, became a Royal Burgh around 1326 during the reign of Robert the Bruce. Its harbour has always been the mainstay of the town, both for fishing and for yachting, and it has adapted with the times to welcome small leisure boats with a mooring pontoon facility. It hosts an annual regatta in May which draws boats from the Clyde coast and further afield. The main Glasgow to Campbeltown road is in the centre of the picture and on the right can be seen the poles or 'crochans' where the fishermen dried their nets. The harbour itself has a distinctive man-made square stone island called the Bielding, which was built to help steer sailing ships into the basin. The shops to the left include A. & D. Shaw, draper and hosier; the Fish and Fruit Market; and a China merchant. A motorist is filling up his car from a petrol pump conveniently placed on the edge of the pavement, common in those days.

The ivy-covered ruins of Tarbert Castle, extended in the fourteenth century from an earlier building, still dominate the town. Although there was a fort recorded on the site as far back as the eighth century, the present castle was enlarged to include a hall, chapel, goldsmith's house, bakery, wine house, mill and lime kiln, and must have been a place of extreme importance. Records from 1326 show that the main masonry contractor was paid £282 (with a bonus because he built the walls wider than originally planned) and the smith, plumber and carpenter were each paid between 2*d* and 4*d* a day for their work. The photograph shows passengers with their cases walking back from the pier after getting off one of the steamers - and although there is a car on the scene, the road shows definite signs that a horse-drawn vehicle has recently passed by!

Harbour Street is Tarbert's main thoroughfare and (as can be seen in the next photograph) was a convenient site to clean and cure freshly caught herring when the boats came in. Tarbert Hotel, pictured here, was just one of several hotels catering for the growing number of tourists at the start of the twentieth century. A gazetteer of Scotland written in the 1880s describes Tarbert as 'a village which is inhabited mainly by fishermen, and is the resort during the herring fishing season of several hundreds of fishermen from other parts. All over the inner space of the loch may be seen in the season a very numerous fleet of herring boats. On the south side of the loch is a steamboat quay where steamers from Glasgow and Ardrishaig call regularly.' The memorial fountain was donated in 1910 by a Mr Millar, who lived in Barmore Road, as a goodwill gesture to the town. It was removed after it was accidentally damaged by a lorry in the 1940s.

Herring gutters on Harbour Street, tackling a catch just landed and emptied into the purpose-built wooden containers known as farlans. The women, who often travelled from east coast fishing villages, worked at top speed, gutting and cleaning the fish in all weathers. The tips of their fingers were bound with strips of cloth to protect them from the often freezing conditions and the salt when the fish were packed into barrels. As this was piece work, they worked non-stop to make a better wage.

In *Tarbert Past and Present* (published in 1886), Dugald Mitchell wrote, 'Regarding hotel accommodation, a very necessary feature in the equipment of a coast village, it is ample. The principal hotel is the "Tarbert", and here under the genial and homely management of Mrs McLean, who has been so long at the head of it, the wayfarer finds himself as comfortable and well tended as it is possible to be away from his ain fireside.' The smart horse-drawn carriage and line-up of the staff suggest the arrival of rather up-market guests. Other hotels in Tarbert at that time were the Victoria and the Commercial (which was later called the Castle Hotel and is now the Islay Frigate Hotel).

The P.S. *Columba*, seen here at Tarbert pier, was the most majestic and best known of all the Clyde passenger steamers. Built by J. & G. Thomson in 1878 and owned by MacBrayne's, she was on the Tarbert and Ardrishaig run, popularly known as the 'Royal Route' as it was often used by the high society of the times *en route* to shooting and fishing in the Highlands. The *Columba* had a post office on board, which was unique among the Clyde steamers, and her fittings included a barber's shop and a smoking room on the promenade deck. She was finally retired and sold for scrap in March 1936.

Golfing fashions may have changed from the 1930s when plus-fours and sensible tweeds were the order of the day, but Tarbert's nine-hole golf course, which was opened in the 1920s, is still very popular with both visitors and locals. This photograph shows the present Glenralloch course near the West Loch, but there was an earlier course on the south side of the village, which was opened around 1905. Local memory records that it started at the Columba Hotel and finished at the Tarbert Hotel, ideal for the thirsty golfer.

Tarbert's first 'recreational grounds pavilion' was opened in April 1901, but it was later replaced by this larger two-storey building which catered for both the bowling green and tennis courts. This in its turn was made redundant and replaced in the 1990s by a modern clubhouse. The original pavilion was dismantled and rebuilt at the golf course, where it served for many years as changing rooms and club storage. When a new golf clubhouse was built about 25 years ago, the pavilion was moved again when it was sold to a resident near the West Loch and re-sited in the grounds of his house.

The Loch Fyne fishing fleet, pictured here around 1905, gives an indication of the vital part that fishing played in Kintyre, not only for the economy but as a whole way of life. These boats are Loch Fyne skiffs, which were first built in the early 1880s and were instantly recognisable by the slope to their masts which were set forward to give maximum space for the men to haul in their catch. The registration letters on the sails are GK for Greenock and AG for Ardrishaig; the Tarbert registration of TT did not come into existence until 1907, when Tarbert was recognised as the headquarters of the Loch Fyne fishing district rather than Ardrishaig. By the beginning of the twentieth century, ring-netting (a team effort between two boats to encircle shoals of fish) had taken over from the more passive drift-netting. A herring-buyer steamer can be seen and it would have remained at anchor until the night's fishing began. The skiffs (some specially adapted for racing and some using standard working sails) were also used for fiercely competitive regattas at Tarbert, Campbeltown and Ayr, where the skill and stamina of both skipper and crew determined the winners.

This photograph of West Loch Tarbert appeared on a postcard sent in 1944, carrying the cryptic message, 'Could you please send sock and pink slipper in Burberry pocket. Going to the pictures tonight, only one wireless shop in town.' The historic eighteenth-century inn, the West Loch Hotel (left) - known as the Campbell Arms Hotel until the 1960s - still welcomes visitors today. The West Loch pier is situated half a mile past the inn, and early steamers such as the *Fingal*, *Glencoe* and the first *Lochiel* stopped there in the nineteenth and early twentieth centuries. The *Glencoe* took mail, passengers and cargo to the Western Isles for 85 years before being scrapped in 1931. The West Loch pier was enlarged in the 1960s with the addition of a berthing dolphin and a ramp to accommodate roll-on/roll-off ferries, but Calmac stopped using the pier in the 1970s and moved to nearby Kennacraig. The pier is still used to land fish catches from Jura and Islay.

Two girls take a break beside a Clyde & Campbeltown Shipping Company lorry, somewhere on the Tarbert road. This company had its origins in 1826 when the Campbeltown & Glasgow Steam Packet Joint Stock Company was formed, carrying passengers, mail and a wide range of cargo, including livestock, for more than 100 years. The best known of the 'Company boats' were the *Kintyre*, *Kinloch* and *Davaar* steamers, which made regular trips to and from Greenock, Gourock, Wemyss Bay, Lochranza, Pirnmill, Carradale and Campbeltown. A newspaper report said the *Davaar* was 'fitted with all the latest novelties for the comfort and safety of the passengers, with a beautifully furnished saloon, stateroom and ladies' cabin, and ample accommodation for steerage passengers and officers' quarters.' In March 1937 the company was taken over by Clyde Cargo Steamers Ltd which changed the name to the Clyde & Campbeltown Shipping Company later in the same year. A handwritten note in the corner of the postcard says 'Jean McG, May 1938'.

Whitehouse was originally known as Lagamhullin, Gaelic for 'mill hollow', but the name changed as the use of Gaelic fell out of favour. In 1886 it was described by Dugald Mitchell as 'a snug little village having its post office, schoolhouse, and blacksmith's shop. Like most country hamlets, it has its stream which drives a sawmill, and a pretty little stream it is, as it ripples away towards the sea.' The turreted house on the right was first known as 'The Sheriff's House' (as the local sheriff lived there at one time) and was occupied by one of the Campbell family of Stonefield. It was later occupied by a handloom weaver, Willie Snowdon, who produced fine tweed, travelling rugs and blankets before and after the Second World War. A picturesque village, Whitehouse was painted in oils by Kintyre-born William Mactaggart in 1875; the painting is now in private ownership.

Whitehouse was one of the main stopping points for the mail coach, where letters were deposited before being delivered to Skipness. The house on the left was owned by the Galbraith family, who were related to the famous Canadian-born economist, J.K. Galbraith, who died in 2006. The children are standing in front of the local blacksmith's shop. Whitehouse has a fine war memorial on the green, commemorating those who were killed during the First World War. The memorial was put up by Sir Peter Mackie, owner of Glenreasdale estate above the village and controller of the White Horse whisky distillery in Islay. Sir Peter donated a set of ivory-mounted bagpipes which were played by members of the Argyll and Sutherland Highlanders in action in France, and he also paid the wages of the local estate volunteers for the duration of the war.

The quiet village of Clachan, with its immaculately maintained cottages and gardens, is believed to be the oldest surviving settlement in upper Kintyre and the area round about it is rich in ancient history. One of the most completely preserved Iron Age sites in Scotland is on Dun Skeig, overlooking the village, with the remains of three forts on the same commanding viewpoint. The small village church was built around 1760 on the site of a thirteenth-century Christian chapel and there are also several mediaeval graveslabs preserved in the churchyard. Nearby Balinakill House, once the home of Sir William Mackinnon, is now a country house hotel. Sir William had been a vehement opponent of the slave trade, and was a friend of the famous explorers David Livingstone and Henry Morton Stanley; indeed Stanley attended his funeral in Clachan in 1893.

Rhunahaorine Point to the north of Tayinloan, a low-lying shingle beach pointing out to the Sound of Gigha, was the scene of a military engagement in 1647 when an army of Covenanters led by Lieutenant-general David Leslie outnumbered and defeated a Royalist army under the command of Lieutenant-general Sir Alexander MacDonald. Some of the Royalists escaped to Ireland, but the remainder fled down Kintyre and were soon after massacred at Dunaverty, Southend. The 1851 census showed 34 houses in Rhunahaorine with 138 villagers, and there were three schools, run by the Church of Scotland, the Free Church, and the Adventure School. The school and schoolhouse pictured, originally the Church of Scotland's, have since been modernised. The area has been designated a Site of Special Scientific Interest by Scottish Natural Heritage and is an important feeding location for several species of grey geese, particularly the rare Greenland white-fronted geese.

The Campbeltown to Tarbert mail coach with its smartly coloured livery and team of horses was on the road from 1871 until 1913 and was said to be the last stage to run in Scotland before motor transport took over. Passengers sat inside or sometimes (as this photograph shows) on the top with the driver, luggage and the mail. The daily journey from Campbeltown Cross to Tarbert pier, stopping at villages on the way up and down the peninsula, was measured precisely at 38 ¾ miles and the return journey took twelve hours. A 1907 guidebook described it poetically: 'The sight of the brightly painted three-horse coach, with passengers outside and inside, and the mails of His Majesty piled high, dashing along with clank of harness and clatter of hoofs, carries one's imagination pleasantly back to the days of Romance before the star of Watt had risen. The driver of the coach holds an office which is no sinecure; every year he drives the compete distance round the equator.'

Tayinloan still retains its historic old inn, which was one of the main staging posts for the Campbeltown to Tarbert mail coach. By the time this photograph was taken, early cars had begun to appear on the unmetalled road, but apart from the car parked outside the inn, there was not much traffic to be held up by this herd of Highland cattle which had strayed on to the main road from Tarbert. A road from Tayinloan to Carradale was suggested by Campbeltown Town Council in 1925 to help with the unemployment problem in the area, but the scheme was never carried out. Tayinloan's ferry link with Gigha, which was originally a small open rowing boat, still continues as a car and passenger ferry.

This photograph of Ardminish, the only village on the island of Gigha, looks towards the coastline of Kintyre, and shows traditional hay rucks in the centre of the picture. The name Gigha is probably Norse in origin and a popular translation is 'God's island', although another meaning could be 'cleft island'. The island was purchased in March 2002 by the local inhabitants who set up the Isle of Gigha Heritage Trust to manage it. The trust also owns the beautiful gardens of Achamore House, developed by one of the island's former owners, Sir James Horlick, and it is home to many exotic plants including a magnificent selection of azaleas and rhododendrons.

Gigha Parish Church, seen here in the foreground, was built and opened in 1923 to replace the previous building of 1780. It contains some fine stained-glass windows, including one commemorating the Rev. Kenneth McLeod (minister in Gigha from 1923 to 1948) who wrote the words of the Scottish march 'The Road to the Isles', and two small windows dedicated to Margaret and Jeannie McNeill, aunts-by-marriage of the author of this book. The ruins of a much earlier mediaeval parish church at Kilchattan, south of Ardminish, still remain along with some intricately carved ancient gravestones. Despite its small size - six miles long and under two miles wide – Gigha has a wealth of archaeological sites, including cairns, standing stones, duns and forts. One of the best known is the ogham stone, marked with symbols from an ancient Celtic language.

This image of Gigha's north-end ferryman is a world away from the modern car ferry which comes into the new pier at the south of the island. The ferryman in 1885, around 20 years before this photograph was taken, was allowed to keep the ferry dues as part of his remuneration along with the Ferry Croft. The dues at that time were '2/- for one passenger, 4/- for a horse, 2/- for a cow, 3*d* a head for sheep, with bulls and stallions double fare'. However, he had to transport the owner of the island (as well as his family, friends, servants and tradesmen) to the mainland free of charge, and if he left the Tayinloan area he had to provide a replacement ferryman at his own expense.

In 1861 Muasdale was described in the book *Glencreggan - Volume 2* as 'a fishing village with one street of one-storey whitewashed cottages thatched with heather, and with two superior houses for the inn and the shop. A tall chimney and lines of sheds, now deserted, was once a Farina Mill, erected for the manufacture of starch from potatoes; this proved a total failure, unfortunately for the people of the district. The inn still flourishes, as it did in the days when it was supported by the fourteen farmers of Muasdale, who were boon companions fond of each other and fonder still of whisky.' The book then tells the story that the fourteen farmers tried to count their number to see if they had all returned after a good day out at Campbeltown fair, but as each forgot to include himself in the count they were always one short of the total. Muasdale remained a fishing village into the twentieth century and was one of the last strongholds of native Gaelic in Kintyre.

This image of Cleit near Muasdale shows the isle of Gigha in the background and a West Coast Motors bus from Clachan parked outside the church at the end of the road. In 1770 the Rev. Robert Thomson had a dream one Saturday night that the parish church at Killean would fall down. On the following day, he was preaching to the assembled crowd outside in the graveyard when the west wall of the old thatched church did indeed fall in, but luckily with no loss of life. A discussion was held on where the new church would be sited and the Duke of Argyll decreed that it must be built at Cleit as this was the centre of the parish. The tenants of MacDonald of Largie said they would rather emigrate than walk the two extra miles from Killean to Cleit, and many did in fact give up their tenancies on this issue and went to a new life in North Carolina. The church took 20 years to build, and the congregation worshipped under the elements until it was completed in 1792 by Thomas Cairns. The school and schoolhouse were built in 1861 and the stables and houses in 1881 by Charles Macalister of Glenbarr.

Above: Despite its name, Glenbarr Abbey (formerly known as Barr House) has no religious connections but is in fact an eighteenth-century mansion house with later additions. The house is owned by a branch of the Macalister family and is the clan centre of the Macalisters. Guided tours are available where family memorabilia, patchworks, and gloves worn by Mary, Queen of Scots, are on view. The area around Barr Glen includes cup-and-ring carvings and the glen gives access to Beinn an Tuirc, which at 1,490 feet is the highest hill in Kintyre.

Right: The cottages of Glenbarr village, now bypassed by the main road, pictured around 1920. The village originally had two rows of thatched houses on both sides of the main road, with a meal mill driven by a water wheel. The buildings in the foreground are Glenbarr Temperance Inn and the village shop. The war memorial above the village was built in 1922 by McArthur's stonemasons from Campbeltown and unveiled by Sgt Edward McDonald D.C.M. The address was given by the Archbishop of York, who spent holidays in the area, and the names of those who died were read out by Mrs MacDonald of Largie. At one time a road was planned to cut across the peninsula from Glenbarr to Arnicle, near Carradale, but this was never carried out.

Right: The Argyll Hotel at Bellochantuy was established in 1785 as a coaching inn and made a convenient stopping-off point for passengers on the Campbeltown to Tarbert mail coach. Once owned by the Duke of Argyll, it was originally called the Bellochantuy Hotel. The notice on the hotel spells Bellochantuy with an 'A' - perhaps for ease of pronunciation as it is pronounced 'Ballochantee'. In September 1939, just after the outbreak of war, the hotel was sprayed by machine gun bullets - not, as was first thought, by an enemy plane but by a British pilot testing out his guns regardless of the alarm he was causing.

Left: In June 1945 the *Campbeltown Courier* reported that a mine had been washed ashore near Bellochantuy , blocking the road to traffic, although the early bus from Campbeltown to Glasgow had already passed the scene before the police closed the road in case traffic vibrations set the mine off. Three more drifted ashore near Muasdale, Tayinloan and Westport, and all were defused by a mine disposal team from Greenock. This photograph shows a Raleigh cycle depot opposite the historic church, which was built around 1820 to serve the southern end of the parish. As farming and working populations declined through emigration, the congregations decreased.

Putechan (pronounced 'Pootchecan') was originally spelled several different ways, including Pautuchan, and was a former hunting lodge for the Duke of Argyll. The first bridge built across the burn Allt-na-Dunach ('stream of misfortune') between Killocraw and Putechan was only wide enough for one cart to pass at a time; in 1718, when two funeral processions going in opposite directions met on the bridge, neither party would give way, apparently causing a fight in which one man was killed. To remedy this, the local landowners built another bridge and both can still be seen. Robert Burns's fiancée, 'Highland Mary' Campbell is said to have paused on one of the bridges on her way to visit relatives at Lagalgarve. This image, taken around 1910, shows workmen painting the outside of Putechan Lodge which has been since been converted into a hotel.

There has been a lighthouse at the Mull of Kintyre since 1788, warning shipping to keep well clear of the dangerous stretch of coast with its tidal currents and treacherous sea. Since then the buildings, including the former keepers' houses, have been remodelled several times and the light itself is now automatic. The road from Southend to the Mull drops nearly 1,000 feet in three-quarters of a mile of hairpin bends. Cars have to be left at the top of the cliffs above the lighthouse and walkers who follow the road downwards are rewarded with breathtaking views across to Antrim and Rathlin Island. A memorial cairn commemorates the 29 victims of the Chinook helicopter crash in 1994, and reminders of earlier aircraft wrecks are still to be found on the hillside. About a mile north of the lighthouse are the remains of Balvicar, a remote hamlet which had houses, agricultural outbuildings, a waterwheel and a corn-drying kiln although it was deserted by 1779.

Southend's main street was a quiet place when this photograph was taken in the early 1900s, showing Alex Reid's grocer's shop with the staff posing at the door in their white aprons. The building, which comprised both shop and the house 'Seaview', was built in 1844 to replace an older shop near Dunglas. A 1907 guidebook advertised the shop as 'Grocer and Provision Merchant. Information given regarding apartments. Picture Post Card Emporium.' This was one of many photographs taken by Edward Keith, who opened his well-stocked stationer's shop in Campbeltown in 1902. He was in the habit of hiring a car and taking his family on outings up and down Kintyre to photograph the countryside (often with his children pictured in the foreground for added interest). He then published the pictures as postcards to sell in his shop, which continued to be run by his son until 1976. Further down the road is the parish church of St Blaan, built in 1774 and the third church of that name. The second one was built on the west side of the river when the original on the east was in danger of being washed away. It then fell into disrepair and was eventually replaced by the present building.

Southend has been a popular tourist spot for many years, but the distinctive Art Deco Keil Hotel has been closed since 1992. Completed in 1937, it was only used as a hotel for a short period as it was converted into a hospital in 1939. The building is now derelict and its future is uncertain. In the early years of the twentieth century many of the hotels in the area had their own horse-drawn or motorised brakes for their visitors. An advertisement in a 1907 guidebook for Southend's Argyll Arms Hotel - then under Mrs Gibson's ownership - offered 'Home comforts and excellent cuisine. Fishing, boating, golf, croquet, bathing and billiards. During summer season, brakes await arrival of Campbeltown steamers.' The ruins of Keil House (featured in the next illustration) can still be seen near the old ruined church of Kilcolmkill which, according to tradition, was founded by Columba before his journey to Iona in 563 AD.

Keil House in Southend was built in 1873 by the wealthy merchant James Nicol Fleming, who married Elizabeth Galbraith of North Park, Campbeltown. He was a director of the City of Glasgow Bank, but fled the country before its crash in 1878. He escaped in a ship of the British India Shipping Company (founded by Campbeltown-born Sir William Mackinnon), which was said to have picked him up from Dunaverty Bay. When Fleming returned to Britain, he was arrested and imprisoned for fraud. The house was then bought by another Glasgow merchant, Ninian Stewart. It was later converted into a private boarding school for boys, thanks to a bequest from Sir William, and was used for this purpose until it burned down in 1924. The school was later successfully re-established in Dumbarton. During the Second World War pupils from the relocated school were evacuated to Sir William's home, Balinakill House near Clachan. The ruins of Keil House, which apparently had 365 windows (one for each day of the year), can still be seen.

Lephenstrath Bridge in Southend was built around 1832 to replace an older one which had been damaged (and which no longer stands), but was itself damaged by flood waters in 1868. There was a hamlet adjacent to the bridge where workers on Lephenstrath estate lived, and which in the nineteenth century included an inn and a grocer's shop. The chimney of one of the houses can just be made out on the right of the picture. Two of the houses of the hamlet have been restored and are still occupied.

The popular Muneroy general store and café was opened around the early 1950s by owners Alf and Morag Grumoli, pictured here at the doorway. Originally there were eight tenement houses and a shop on the site, but just after the Second World War grants were made available for rebuilding on the site of old properties on condition that part of the original building was retained. The buildings were demolished apart from the back wall, which was kept as an internal central wall. Part of the old tenement, which had a row of houses behind it in the picturesquely named Teapot Lane, can be seen in the photograph on page 30. Muneroy Stores remains an important part of village life today.

Little now remains of Dunaverty Castle which stood on the headland at Southend for centuries and which was an important stronghold due to its commanding position. It was visited by Robert the Bruce in 1306 and more than a century later by James IV. It was the scene of a massacre in 1647 when some 300 Royalist soldiers were killed after surrendering at the end of a siege by the Covenanting army of Lieutenant-general David Leslie. The bodies were buried in a nearby field. The buildings near the rock were the RNLI station and slip, which opened in 1868. The station's first lifeboat was named the *John R. Ker* in memory of a young man who drowned at Clachan in 1867. A new boathouse with improved launching facilities was opened in August 1905 by the Dowager Duchess of Argyll, with a new lifeboat which was given the same name as the first one. The station closed in 1929; it was converted into a house and the base of the slip is still in place with a modern shed on it. Dunaverty was a popular picnic beach for Campbeltown folk and is now overlooked by a large caravan site.

The island of Sanda, two miles from Southend, is steeped in ancient history. It was from here that the Norwegian King Hacon sent ships to conquer Scotland before being defeated at the Battle of Largs in 1263. Historical remains include remnants of St Ninian's Chapel, an old sandstone cross, a holy well and ancient gravestones. The lighthouse, with its three sandstone towers on the rock face, was established in 1850 and engineered by Alan Stevenson. It was automated in 1992 and the keepers' cottages have been converted into holiday accommodation. The original lighthouse lens is now displayed at Scotland's Lighthouse Museum. An American Liberty ship, the *Byron Darnton*, ran aground on Sanda in 1946 and all 54 people on board were rescued. The ship's name is commemorated in the pub which was recently opened on the island. Sanda was designated a Site of Special Scientific Interest by Scottish Natural Heritage in 1995 and is home to colonies of guillemots, razorbills, puffins and stormy petrels, as well as grey and common seals.

Stewarton, at the junction of the Machrihanish and Southend roads, took its name from the Stewart family who contributed a great deal to the improvement of farming in Kintyre in the late eighteenth and nineteenth centuries. John Lorne Stewart, who succeeded his father Duncan as the Duke of Argyll's Chamberlain of Kintyre from 1829 to 1856, oversaw the change from communal farming to the type of family management still in place today. His obituary in the *Argyllshire Herald* in July 1878 said, 'He farmed Glenaharvie, Tomaig, and the two Knockriochs in a manner superior to anything seen before in the district. On Tomaig, he executed the bold idea of irrigation with potale [a by-product of whisky distilling] and caused what was a poor and barren soil to produce some of the heaviest crops in the district.' Stewart also introduced a new strain of 45 dairy cattle and produced 'imitation English cheese for which he got the highest English prices in the Glasgow markets.' The stone bust on the side of Stewarton General Store which can be seen in this 1920s photograph, and which is still in place, may well be Lorne Stewart, although Robert Burns is also a candidate. One of Kintyre's best-known folk songs, 'Nancy's Whisky', includes the lines, 'As I cam roon by Stewarton corner, It was Nancy's whisky I chanced to spy.'

This rare photograph of the mining village of Drumlemble, near Machrihanish, shows its main street of single-storey cottages or miners' 'raws'. Records show that coal was mined in Drumlemble as early as the seventeenth century. A shaft was sunk in 1798 by the Campbeltown Coal Company and it later became part of the Argyll Colliery, with coal being transported by narrow gauge railway hauled by the *Pioneer* or the *Chevalier* to Campbeltown pier. The pit was directly affected by the General Strike in 1926 and social conditions were so bad after this that eleven families from Drumlemble and Campbeltown emigrated to Western Australia to look for better living conditions. The picture shows the three village schools, with the gable end of one school shown to the right of the picture. The building adjoining it to the left was used as the girls' 'shed' and was originally part of the village brickworks. Another school, up the hill on the right, was run by the Free Church. On the left of the picture is the main Drumlemble school which was in use until the 1950s, with the schoolhouse in front of it.

This photograph of Peninver was taken around 1910 and shows what was then the entire village. Craiglussa, pictured in the centre, was built in 1885 by a salmon fisherman called Thomas Eaglesome, who lived in another cottage in the village before moving to his new home (he also built the jetty). Also pictured, next to Craiglussa on the left, is the post office run for many years by the McMillan family, and the white cottage at the end of the street on the far left of the photograph belonged at one time to New Peninver farm. The lady is standing beside Craigview (later extended to include the village pub, also called Craigview), with the school and schoolhouse adjacent out of shot. A report on the school, made by an inspector for the Scottish Society for the Propagation of Christian Knowledge in 1824, said, 'Few attended this school in summer and 40 attended during the winter. The house and schoolhouse are in good repair and the garden and cows are amply attached. There is no Sabbath evening school and most of the scholars pay fees. The fuel is provided by the teacher William Stewart who has 30 years in the service of the society.'

Right: The village of Saddell, seen here around the 1930s, is dominated by nearby Saddell Castle which was built by the Bishop of Argyll around 1508. Its adjacent farm steadings were added in the seventeenth century, using many of the stones from the ruined abbey nearby. The abbey itself was founded in 1160 by the legendary warrior king Somerled, who was the forefather of the Lords of the Isles, and whose symbolic galley was carved on the entrance to the castle. Important examples of mediaeval Celtic carved gravestones can be seen at Saddell, showing knights in armour, priests in ornate robes, monks, and sailing ships.

Below: Saddell ferry, actually just a small open rowing boat, was run by the Galbraith family from the late nineteenth century and transferred passengers to and from the Campbeltown steamer. The first ferryman was Donald Galbraith, a native of Gigha, and he was followed by his son Lachlan after whom the fishermen named Port na Cuthaig. In an agreement drawn up in 1887, the Galbraiths charged passengers 6*d* each - the same as for sheep or swine - parcels cost 2*d*, wool bags 8*d*, and iron fencing 3/- per ton. They also reserved the right not to board the steamer in stormy weather. A near-fatal accident occurred in January 1896 when Lachlan's sister Flora fell between the ferry and the steamer *Kintyre*; after being under water for some considerable time, she was rescued and pulled to safety.

The pier at Carradale, the centre of the village's fishing industry, was built in 1871 by the then laird, Colonel Buchanan, to replace an earlier one. It was the first iron pier to be built in Scotland, and its unique design on two levels - the lower one to suit fishing boats and the higher level for steamers - can be clearly seen in this photograph with a view looking east to the Arran hills. The R.M.S. *Davaar*, seen approaching the pier, was built in 1885 and originally had two funnels. It was one of the 'Campbeltown Yachts' owned by the Campbeltown & Glasgow Steam Packet Company. The *Davaar* made occasional excursion runs to Belfast and once ran aground on the coast at County Down but was refloated. This photograph dates from around 1925 and the fenders slung over the starboard sides of the Long Fyne skiffs are old car tyres – in earlier times old ropes and netting were used to protect the sides of the boats.

The iron pier at Carradale, *c.* 1910. Steamers which arrived here carried not only tourists and locals, but also necessities such as machinery, livestock and heavy household items which were more easily transported by water than by the twisting road from Campbeltown. A porter, waiting with a barrow to transport visitors' luggage, can be seen in the centre of the picture. The large lidded wooden herring boxes at the side of the pier held about half a cran of fish and were known as 'Glasgow boxes'. This pier was dismantled and a new one completed in 1959, and the village is still home to a depleted fishing fleet, now mainly catching scallops and other shellfish.

This was the original post office in Carradale, and the building also contained a shop on the left and a house in the centre. The business was acquired by Keith Campbell around 1886, when mail was collected from the steamer at Carradale pier and taken up to the post office for sorting and then delivery. On his death it was taken over by his son Donald, and finally run by Donald's sons Keith and Walter until they retired in 1988. The building in the photograph was demolished and the Glen bar and restaurant was built on the site in 1971.

The Bungalow shop and tearoom stood on 'The Brae' leading down to Carradale harbour, and was run by the Ritchie family from around the late 1920s. This image belongs to a time when Carradale was a thriving holiday resort and the fishing families made a good supplementary living by letting their houses to visitors during the summer while they themselves lived in the outhouses. As in other parts of the country, the domestic holiday trade declined in the post-war period when cheap foreign air travel became the norm. The Bungalow was demolished and a house known by the same name has been built on the site.

Between 1887 and 1891 this building was used as Carradale's infant school, as it was thought that the main school in Carradale Glen was too far for young children to travel. The minutes of the school board stated that it was 'agreeable that an infant school for children under seven years of age and conducted by a duly certificated female teacher should be erected at some suitable position near the post office.' The small building probably held between 12 and 15 youngsters, with 84 older children attending the main school. The building later became a house, a Forestry Commission visitor centre, and now forms part of the Network Heritage Centre which gives information about the fishing, farming and forestry of the area. The Forestry Commission's Deer Hill trail now has its western end here.

Now part of Carradale, Airds village was not only a separate hamlet when this photograph was taken in the early 1900s, but was divided into three parts - High, Mid and - pictured - Low Airds. The cottages on the right have their front doors at the back - said to be because they were built for estate workers by the laird who didn't want to see any washing hanging next to the village street. Neil Sinclair Stalker, who took a day trip from Campbeltown on the *Davaar* in 1902, wrote, 'Three of us arrived at Carradale pier, and were rather surprised on being asked to pay twopence each. My friend however, who knew the lad at the toll-gate, placed twopence in his outstretched palm, and all three of us walked past. We then walked through the village of Airds, our ears being greeted at every turn by the guttural sound of the Gaelic. After walking over an old fashioned moss-grown bridge we went to see our friend the smith. Upon entering the smithy, some of the burning sparks caught me rather unexpectedly.' The name Airds comes from the Gaelic for a height or promontory, and the remains of Airds Castle can still be seen 400 metres south of the harbour.

Grogport had two fishing skiffs in the early 1900s: John McAllister's *Effie* (CN230) and Samuel Conley's *Martha* (CN162). About the same period, local shopkeeper Colin Campbell (known as 'Colin Grogport') sold provisions through neighbouring Carradale in a horse and buggy. His cry was, 'Syrup an' treacle! Sausages an' cream crackers! Dae ye want any?' Grogport also had an old inn which was well patronised when Carradale had no licensed premises, with men walking six miles there and back for a dram. The remains of a nearby Neolithic cist (stone box) grave, known locally as 'The Sailor's Grave', probably dates back more than 4,000 years.

Claonaig was once seen as the centre of the parish of Saddell and Skipness, and its parish church was built in 1756. The shooting lodge, which was rented out by tenants, was originally a prefabricated wooden building with the materials shipped over from Norway by sea and landed on the beach. Claonaig is now best known as the Kintyre port of call for the Calmac ferry service to and from Lochranza in Arran.

RN CRUISERS IN FOCUS

Lt Cdr Ben Warlow RN

EDITOR'S NOTES

This edition of Maritime Books "Focus" series covers the Royal Navy's cruisers through World War I to their disappearance at the end of the 20th Century. Their name- cruisers – does not sound as belligerent as 'battleship' or 'destroyer', but they were major assets in the Royal Navy's arsenal. They lived up to their name in that they were 'long legged', able to cruise long distances in their duties of protecting commerce throughout the oceans of the World. Equipped with workshops and carrying artisans, they were self reliant for maintenance, not needing Fleet Maintenance Units to be sent out to assist them. In their crew was a complete range of all the skills required for self-reliance, including doctors and dentists. Later ships were able to steam comfortably at high speeds using one set of machinery, whilst their other set was being maintained. They were not powerful enough to be placed in the line of battle with capital ships, as was demonstrated so tragically at Jutland. Never the less they carried a powerful main armament, which could deter raiders from attacking convoys, and which could be put to invaluable service in precision shore bombardment in support of the Army. They also had the capacity to carry large numbers of troops at high speed. In World War II they often provided the best anti-aircraft cover for convoys and military operations ashore, especially the smaller C class AA conversions and the light Dido class. Cruisers were frequently in the thick of the fighting and there were never enough of them.

Great Britain and the Commonwealth had just 65 cruisers at the outbreak of World War II. Thirty two (3 of which were of the Royal Australian Navy) were war losses, and only 29 new cruisers were completed during the war – of which 25 had been laid down prior to the end of 1939. It had been fortunate that the shipbuilding programme had been speeded up prior to the outbreak of the war. With so few ships, it was inevitable that they should often be required to 'fight above their weight', as happened at the River Plate. Sometimes, though, skill and courage were insufficient qualities to balance the enemy's superior numbers, as in the Java Sea when EXETER and PERTH were overwhelmed. Cruisers were not immune to air attack, and incurred damage and loss whilst defending the convoys or the Army. Casualties were often high – SYDNEY, no survivors, NEPTUNE, just one, GLOUCESTER over 700 lost. I hope that the captions in this book show some of the diversity of their employment. Cruisers were excellent command ships, and generally well balanced fighting ships. More-over, in my opinion, and I hope yours after seeing these photographs, these were some of the handsomest ships ever built and were well suited to 'showing the Flag' operations during the piping days of peace. It is hard to understand why a Navy, which has given up so many bases overseas, does not have any of these ships remaining in its Fleet.

Ben Warlow
Burnham-on-Crouch
2003

> For Patrick, Oli and Alex
> Who will never have the good fortune to see these
> magnificent ships at sea

Note: All photographs are from the author's collection except where indicated. 'PRNM' denotes Portsmouth Royal Naval Museum, which includes photographs from the Wright and Logan and A and J Pavia Collections, "IWM" denotes Imperial War Museum, 'MPL' denotes Maritime Photo Library.

First published in the United Kingdom in 2003 by Maritime Books, Lodge Hill, Liskeard, Cornwall, PL14 4EL

HMS DRAKE

Britain built armoured cruisers towards the end of the 19th Century to counter French, German and Russian developments, particularly in the building of fast cruisers for commerce raiding. A typical example was the Drake class, enlarged in size over their predecessors to permit more engine power, developing 23 knots. DRAKE was armed with two 9.2-inch and sixteen 6-inch guns, and was completed in December 1903, achieving 24.11 knots on trials. These ships proved good sea-boats with exceptional steadiness. In the Great War DRAKE served in the Grand Fleet and later was employed escorting convoys in the Atlantic. She was torpedoed by U-79 on 2 October 1917 off the North Coast of Ireland. Still able to steam, she made for Rathlin Island, where she anchored, but later capsized and sank. 19 of her crew were lost.

HMS MONMOUTH

Whilst large armoured cruisers were being built with an eye to employing them with the Fleet, the Monmouth class was intended for trade protection. As fast as the Drake class, they were less well armed and protected. They carried fourteen 6-inch guns. The forward and after guns were in twin turrets, whose weight caused the ships to pitch in a seaway. SUFFOLK achieved 24.7 knots on trials and KENT reached 25 knots during a chase of the German cruiser DRESDEN. MONMOUTH was completed in December 1903 and served in home waters and on the China Station before the Great War. In October 1914 she joined in the search for a German cruiser force off South America. She was lost with all hands when engaged by the German NURNBERG during the action off Coronel (Chile) on 1 November 1914, sinking with her flag bravely flying.

HMS DEFENCE
The development of the heavy cruiser continued, with their armament becoming progressively heavier. The Minotaur class, with a displacement of 14,600 tons and an armament of 9.2-inch guns in twin turrets fore and aft, and 7.5-inch guns in turrets along their sides, were the last of these ships. DEFENCE was completed in February 1909, and achieved 22.9 knots on trials. She was with the Grand Fleet at Jutland as Admiral Arbuthnott's Flagship. Over-gunned at the expense of protection, DEFENCE came under fire from the German battleship FRIEDRICH DER GROSSE and was lost with all 893 of her crew.

HMS CALYPSO (July 1935)

Light cruisers were developed to work with destroyer flotillas on scouting duties. They were fast and manoeuvrable, and were powerful enough to defend their flotillas against enemy surface craft. Their design was developed throughout the pre-war and Great War years, and the Caledon class were the oldest cruisers to survive into the Second World War. Designed to hunt down German destroyers in the North Sea, they were called upon to serve world –wide. The Caledons introduced the straight, cutaway bow and carried their torpedo tubes on the upper deck instead of submerged. CALYPSO was completed in June 1917. She was damaged by shell-fire in an action in the Heligoland Bight. In September 1939 she joined the Northern Patrol and in December 1940 transferred to the Mediterranean, where, on 12 June 1940, she became the first casualty of the war in the Mediterranean when she was torpedoed by the Italian submarine ALPINO BAGNOLINI South of Crete. She was lost before plans to modernise her in line with her sisters could be implemented.   (MPL)

HMS CARADOC

CARADOC was completed in June 1917. Between the wars she served in the Mediterranean, the China Station and the America and West Indies Station before becoming a training ship in August 1938. In September 1939 she covered the transfer of the British Expeditionary Force to France and in October intercepted a German supply ship, which scuttled herself. She then joined the Eastern Fleet. In June 1943 she became a Gunnery Training Ship at Durban and in March 1944 became a base ship for escort forces at Colombo. She was placed in reserve in November 1945 and broken up in April 1946. CALEDON of this class was modernised with twin 4-inch guns for AA work in line with ships of the later C class groups.

(MPL)

HMS CARDIFF (July 1935)
The next group of light cruisers were fitted with their second 6-inch gun forward of the bridges, which were higher and further aft. This greatly improved sea-keeping and arcs of fire. CARDIFF was completed on 25 June 1917. She joined the Light Cruiser Squadron attached to the battlecruisers and was in the action in the Heligoland Bight in November 1917. A year later she led the German Fleet to their surrender. She served in the Baltic and the Mediterranean, African and China Stations between the wars. In 1939 she undertook Northern Patrols and in January 1940 became the Gunnery Firing and experimental ship at Portsmouth. She covered the bombardment of Cherbourg in October 1940 and later that month became based on the Clyde. She paid off in July 1945 and was handed over to be broken up in March 1946.

(PRNM)

HMS CURLEW (May 1937)

CURLEW was completed in December 1917. Between the wars she served world wide, including taking part in the Empire cruise 1923-24. She underwent a prototype conversion to an AA cruiser at Chatham 1935-36, with a main armament of ten single 4-inch guns, as seen here. In August 1939 she was fitted with the first production (as distinct from experimental) radar set to go to sea. The next month she undertook AA duties escorting convoys to and from Norway. In April and May 1940 she provided AA cover at Namsos and Aandalsnes (Norway), and on 26 May 1940, while in Lavang Fjord, she came under air attack. Four bombs exploded beneath her machinery spaces, her side was split and she lost all power. She anchored and was abandoned with her quarterdeck awash. She capsized and sank 2$\frac{1}{2}$ hours after the attack and her wreck was depth charged to destroy the radar aerials. (MPL)

HMS CURACOA (1935)

This photograph (and the next on page 11) shows the major conversion undertaken to fit these ships for the AA role. CURACOA was built at Pembroke Dockyard and was completed in February 1918. In May 1919 she was damaged by a mine during operations in the Baltic. She served in the Mediterranean before becoming a tender to the Gunnery School at Portsmouth in 1932.

(MPL)

HMS CURACOA (August 1942)

CURACOA underwent an AA conversion at Chatham from 1939-40. Her new design was a development from the prototype conversions (see CURLEW page 9 and COVENTRY page 13), in that she was fitted with four twin 4-inch guns, a four barreled pom-pom and two multiple machine guns. In April 1940 she carried troops to Molde (Norway) and remained to provide AA cover. She was damaged on 24 April 1940 and was towed back to UK by the sloop FLAMINGO. In August 1940 she began ocean escort duties. On 2 October 1942 she was escorting RMS QUEEN MARY and was sunk in a collision with her 20 miles North West of Bloody Foreland (Eire). 338 of her crew were lost.

(IWM Neg No: A10645)

HMS COVENTRY

COVENTRY was built as a light cruiser by Swan Hunter and completed in 1918 with five 6-inch guns, as is shown in this photograph. She was also temporarily fitted with a flying off platform amidships, the only one of the class to be fitted to carry aircraft. She served in the Harwich Force in the Great War, and afterwards in the Atlantic and Mediterranean. In 1935-6 she was refitted at Portsmouth as a prototype AA cruiser armed with a main armament of ten single 4-inch AA guns similar to CURLEW (see page 9). The next photograph shows her with war modifications.

HMS COVENTRY (June 1940)

COVENTRY was recalled from the Mediterranean to home waters in October 1939. She was damaged by near misses during the Norwegian campaign. In August 1940 she covered convoys in the Red Sea and Eastern Mediterranean. She was damaged by a torpedo from the Italian submarine NEGHELLI in December 1940, but continued to operate despite having no bow below her waterline. In April 1941 she took part in the evacuation of Greece, and the next month was damaged by a near miss off Crete. Repairs in Bombay had to wait until October 1941, meanwhile she remained operational. After being repaired she took part in an unsuccessful attempt to run a convoy to Malta from the East. On 14 September 1942, whilst trying to cover the destroyers ZULU and SIKH during an assault on Tobruk, she came under heavy aircraft attack and was badly hit. She had to be sunk by ZULU.

HMS COLOMBO

The next group of light cruisers were fitted with 'trawler' bows to reduce spray and wetness, and this made them 18 inches longer. None were completed before the Great War ended. COLOMBO was built by Fairfield, being launched in December 1918 and completed in June 1919. She served on the China, East Indies, America and West Indies and Mediterranean Stations between the wars. In 1939 she was on Northern Patrols and in March 1940 transferred to the East Indies. She escorted troop convoys and returned to Devonport for an AA conversion from June 1942 to June 1943. (This photograph shows her pre-conversion appearance). She then joined the Mediterranean Fleet for the invasion of Sicily, then undertook convoy work. She was at the invasion of the South of France and then carried out bombardments in the Aegean. In May 1945 she returned to UK and was placed in reserve. She was broken up in 1948.

HMS CALCUTTA

CALCUTTA was completed in August 1918. She served on the America and West Indies Station to 1927, then the Africa Station to 1931. This pre-conversion photograph shows clearly the layout of her five 6-inch guns. Placed in reserve, she was later converted to an AA cruiser in 1939-40. She was AA ship at Scapa Flow, then took part in Northern Patrols before providing AA cover at Loch Ewe. During the Norwegian campaign she was at Namsos, Aandalsnes and Narvik. In May she was at Dunkirk and rescued 1856 troops. During later evacuations from France she was in collision with HMCS FRASER, which sank. After a refit she joined the Mediterranean Fleet, escorting convoys and supporting the Army in Libya. In April 1941 she was at the evacuation of Greece, and the next month at Crete. She was lost to air attack in the Eastern Mediterranean on 1 June 1941 when en route to escort the last of the evacuating forces. She sank in 5 minutes with the loss of 118 of her crew.

HMS CAIRO

CAIRO was launched on 19 November 1918 at Birkenhead and completed in October 1919. This pre-conversion view shows the trawler bow peculiar to this group. She served world wide between the wars, and was converted to an AA cruiser from 1938-1939. In 1939 she was employed on trade protection. During the Norwegian campaign she took a convoy to Narvik and covered the landings at Harstad. On 5 May 1940 she was damaged by a near miss, repairs taking until August 1940. She then covered convoys in Home waters and visited Russia. In April 1942 she transferred to the Mediterranean to support operations ferrying aircraft to Malta. In June 1942 she was escort to the Harpoon convoy to Malta during which she was damaged by Italian cruisers. In July 1942 she covered further aircraft ferry operations for Malta. On 12 August 1942, whilst escorting the (Pedestal) convoy to Malta, she was torpedoed by the Italian Submarine AXUM. Her stern was blown off and she had to be sunk by the other escorts.

HMS DANAE (1930)

The next group of light cruisers, the D Class, were 20 feet longer, and incorporated an extra 6-inch gun abaft their bridge. DANAE, the first of the class, completed on 22 June 1918, and was unusual in having neither a trawler bow nor any capability to carry aircraft. In 1923-24 she was part of the Special Service Squadron that carried out a World cruise. In January 1925 she commissioned for the Mediterranean, and was detached to the China Station for a spell. In 1929 she joined the America and West Indies Squadron and later returned to the China Station. In the Second World War she operated mainly in eastern waters. In 1944 she took part in the Normandy landings and from October 1944 was lent to the Polish Navy for a year, being renamed CONRAD. She was sold to T.W. Ward in 1948 for scrapping.

HMS DAUNTLESS
DAUNTLESS and DRAGON, the second and third members of the class, were completed in 1918 to a revised design to incorporate an aircraft hangar under their bridges. This photograph shows the hangar in DAUNTLESS, with her bridge raised above it. These hangars were later removed. Neither ship had a trawler bow. DAUNTLESS was completed on 2 December 1918 on the Tyne. She took part in the Empire Cruise 1923-24 and was badly damaged by grounding in 1928 off Halifax, Nova Scotia.

HMS DAUNTLESS (14 May 1942)

This photograph shows DAUNTLESS during World War II, with her hangar removed, and extra AA guns and radar fitted. In October 1939 she sailed to the China Station via the Mediterranean and undertook patrols and convoy duty. She returned to the UK in January 1942, and in March 1942 joined the Eastern Fleet, escorting troop convoys. In March 1943 she was in the Persian Gulf but 3 months later she returned to the UK and was employed as a training ship, based on Rosyth. She remained in that role until February 1946, when she was paid off. She was broken up in that year.

HMS DELHI

DELHI completed in June 1919. The fourth member of the class, she was fitted with a trawler bow and with a platform for aircraft amidships, a pattern followed by the remaining four of the class. The aircraft arrangements were removed in the late 1920s. DELHI served widely before the war, on the Mediterranean and American Stations as well as taking part in the 1923-24 World cruise. She was completing a refit when war started and then served on the Home Station, intercepting two German merchant ships in October and November 1939. She then served with the Mediterranean Fleet and the South Atlantic Command, with a short spell in Force H in July 1940.

HMS DELHI (3 April 1942)

In May 1941 DELHI arrived at Brooklyn, the first RN ship to be refitted (as distinct from repaired) in the USA. She was re-armed with five US style 5-inch guns with modern AA fire control systems, and given an increased endurance. The refit completed in December 1941, and her resulting distinctive appearance is clear in this photograph. She then served in Home Waters and in the Mediterranean, taking part in the landings in North Africa, where she was hit aft by a bomb. After repairs, she returned to the Mediterranean for the landings in Sicily, Salerno, Anzio and the South of France. In November 1944 she became AA guard-ship at Split. On 12 February 1945 she was damaged when an unmanned explosive motor boat hit a landing craft alongside her. Repairs were abandoned and she was laid up in Falmouth in July 1945. After ship target trials she was broken up in March 1948.

HMS DUNEDIN (23 May 1937)

This broadside view shows the layout of the six single 6-inch guns fitted in the D Class cruisers. DUNEDIN was completed in October 1919. She took part in the Empire Cruise 1923-24, and transferred to the New Zealand Division in 1924 in place of the CHATHAM, remaining with that Division until 1937, when she was relieved by the LEANDER. She was then placed in reserve at Portsmouth. When war began she served in home waters and in the Atlantic, capturing a German auxiliary in July 1941. On 24 November 1941 she was sunk by U-124 in mid Atlantic. Although many of her crew reached the liferafts, it was 78 hours before they were discovered, by which time all but 72 had died, and five more died within a day of being rescued. Over 400 were lost.

(World Ship Photo Library)

HMS DURBAN

DURBAN was launched at Greenock on 29 May 1919 and was completed at Devonport on 31 October 1921. This quarter view shows the third 4-inch AA gun mounted abaft the fifth 6-inch (X) gun, the other two being each side amidships. Their lack of AA armament made these ships unsuitable for operations with an air threat, but they were useful for commerce protection in deep waters. DURBAN served World wide between the wars. In 1939 she served in the South Atlantic and later on the China Station. She escorted reinforcements to Singapore and in February 1942 was damaged by Japanese aircraft off Singapore. Repairs were carried out at Colombo, New York and Portsmouth, taking to July 1942. She then rejoined the Eastern Fleet, returning to the UK in November 1943. She was refitted as a blockship and on 9 June 1944.she was expended as a part of the artificial harbour during the Normandy operation.

HMS DIOMEDE (1920s)

DIOMEDE was launched on 29 April 1919 by Vickers, Barrow, and completed on 7 October 1922 at Portsmouth. The last of her class, she carried her forward 6-inch gun in a turret (Mk XVI). She was on the China Station 1922-25 and then served with the New Zealand Division from 1925 to 1936. In 1939 she took part in the Northern Patrol and in March 1940 was in the South Atlantic, and later that year operated in the West Indies. In December she intercepted a German merchant ship, which scuttled herself. For a period in 1941-42 she operated with US forces, at times under US operational control. In June 1942 she returned to the UK for a refit, which lasted to May 1943. During that refit her torpedo tubes were removed an extra accommodation provided for her new role as a training ship in the Forth area. She paid off in September 1945 and was broken up in 1946.

(MPL)

HMS EMERALD (1928)

The next group of light cruisers were 100 feet longer than the D class to incorporate engines developing twice the power. They also mounted a seventh 6-inch gun. They had a sheer forward rather than a trawler bow, as can be seen in this photograph of EMERALD. She was launched on the Tyne in 1920 and completed at Chatham in 1925. She achieved 32.9 knots on trials. Most of her pre-war service was spent on the East Indies Station. In 1939 she served on the Northern Patrol, and in the Atlantic. In October 1940 she took part in a bombardment of Cherbourg. A few days later she and NEWCASTLE engaged four German destroyers at long range in a chase that reached 32.5 knots. She took part in the occupation of E. African ports, and in 1942 was with the Eastern Fleet during the Japanese advance towards India. She was a bombarding ship for the Normandy landings, during which she was damaged in an air attack. After repairs, she was placed in reserve and then was used for trials before being broken up in July 1948.   (MPL)

25

HMS ENTERPRISE (January 1944)

ENTERPRISE was launched on 23 December 1919 on the Clyde and was completed at Devonport in March 1926. She was fitted with a twin 6-inch gun forward (Mk XVII) and given a new style bridge with a prototype gunnery director on it - in place of the old spotting top and range finder. Her Kingfisher aircraft can be seen abaft the after funnel. Between the wars she served on the China Station and in the East Indies. She took part in the Norwegian campaign in 1940, and in June 1940 joined Force H and was at the action off Calabria. Later she joined the East Indies Fleet and rescued survivors from the CORNWALL and DORSETSHIRE in April 1942. Returning to home waters, she and GLASGOW engaged eleven German destroyers and torpedo boats in December 1943, Z27, T25 and T26 being sunk. In June 1944 she bombarded Utah beach, firing over 4,000 rounds of 6-inch. In October 1944 she was placed in reserve, and was used for trooping before being broken up in April 1946.

(IWM Neg No: A21139)

HMS HAWKINS

HAWKINS was completed in July 1919. She had a heavy armament of seven 7.5-inch guns. She had a good speed (29.5 knots) and radius of action and was designed with two sets of boilers so that she could operate far from regular bases and use either coal of fuel oil. The coal-fired boilers were removed in 1928. In the mid-1930s she was demilitarised and used as a boys' training ship. At the outbreak of war she was re-armed with her original seven 7.5-inch guns. She joined the South Atlantic Station in early 1940 for escort duties and to search for raiders. In 1941 she helped capture ports in East Africa and also captured Axis merchant ships. She later joined the Eastern Fleet for escort duties. In March 1944 she returned to the UK and was in the bombarding force for the Normandy landings in the American sector. She then became a training ship again. She was placed in reserve in June 1945, she was later used for bombing trials before being handed over for breaking up in 1947.

HMS VINDICTIVE

VINDICTIVE was launched as the CAVENDISH in January 1918 by Harland and Wolff. Her name was changed in June 1918 to commemorate the cruiser of Zeebrugge fame. Although the first of the class to complete, she emerged as an aircraft carrier on the lines of the FURIOUS. The superfiring 7.5-inch guns were not fitted, and B gun deck became a flying-off platform with wind-breaking palisades, whilst derricks, and a large flight deck for flying off aircraft were fitted abaft her funnels. She was completed too late to be tried under wartime conditions. She ran aground during operations in the Baltic in 1919. Used for trooping duties in the early 1920's, she was converted to her original cruiser role at Chatham in 1923-25, but retained her forward hangar. From 1930-33 she was used for trooping and carried out catapult trials in late 1935.

HMS VINDICTIVE

In 1936 VINDICTIVE was converted again, this time to a training ship with a token armament and a single funnel, as is seen here. She relieved her sister ship FROBISHER from August 1937. In August 1938 she was converted at Devonport, this time to a repair ship. She served in the Norwegian campaign and later operated in the South Atlantic and Mediterranean, being at Malta from January until October 1944, when she became based on Scapa Flow. She paid off to reserve in August 1945 and was sold the next year.

(Steve Bush Collection)

HMS RALEIGH

RALEIGH was launched by Beardmore at Dalmuir on 28 August 1919 and steamed to Devonport in September 1920 to complete there on 15 April 1921. Her machinery was upgraded to develop 70,000-shaft horse-power (earlier ships of the class having just 60,000-shaft horse-power) and she achieved 31 knots on trials. Completed too late to carry out their designed function of countering German large light cruisers and commerce raiders on the High Seas, these ships proved to be a sound design for future heavy cruiser development. By 1936 their 7.5-inch guns had been removed with a view to their replacement by 6-inch weapons to conform to International Treaty. However, only EFFINGHAM was so modified, the others being re-armed with 7.5-inch as the situation demanded/permitted due to the advent of the war.

(MPL)

HMS RALEIGH (1926)

RALEIGH commissioned for the North America and West Indies Station on 23 July 1921, a delay caused by manpower shortages. She arrived at Bermuda in August and carried out cruises around Canada and the USA. Unfortunately she ran aground in the Straits of Belle Isle on 8 August 1922 in thick fog. She was badly holed and flooded, and her crew reached shore on rafts and lifelines. It was found impossible to re-float her and her equipment was salvaged where possible, and the wreck used for target practice in 1926 by CAPETOWN. This sad scene shows her after the first day of firing, with her masts gone. In 1927 teams from the CALCUTTA blew up what remained of her hull.

HMS FROBISHER

FROBISHER was launched at Devonport on 29 September 1924 and commissioned on 3 January 1925 for the Mediterranean Station. In 1927 she was detached to China and in March 1927 helped destroy 40 pirate junks at Fanto Kong Inlet. She returned to the Mediterranean and in 1929 served in the Atlantic. From 1932 she was converted to a Cadets' Training Ship at Portsmouth (as seen in this photograph), filling that role to July 1937 when she was relieved by her sister ship, VINDICTIVE. In June 1939 she was taken in hand for re-armament, but did not commission until January 1942, when she joined the Eastern Fleet. In February 1944 she joined the Home Fleet and took part in the Normandy bombardments. On 8 August 1944 she was damaged by a German circling torpedo. After repairs and modifications, she became the Cadets' Training Ship. In June 1947 she was relieved by the DEVONSHIRE, paid off to reserve and was eventually broken up in 1949.

HMS EFFINGHAM (June 1938)

EFFINGHAM was built by Portsmouth Dockyard being completed on 9 July 1925. Both she and FROBISHER were completed with 10 oil-fired boilers only, developing 65,000-shaft horse-power. After seven years in the East Indies she was placed in reserve. In 1937she was modernised. Her main armament was replaced by nine single 6-inch guns, the forward three being mounted in tiers ahead of her bridge, a layout repeated with the Dido Class. Her two after boilers were removed and the uptakes for the remainder were trunked into a single funnel. In 1939 she undertook Atlantic escort duty and in March 1940 she took bullion across the Atlantic. In April and May 1940 she operated off the Norwegian coast to protect landings, search for enemy destroyers, and carry out bombardments. On 17 May she embarked a battalion of troops at Harstad for Bodo. Unfortunately the next day she ran aground in sight of Bodo between Briksvaer and the Terra Islands and could not be re-floated. Her troops, stores and crew were taken off and she was destroyed by torpedoes from the MATA-BELE.

(PRNM)

HMS ADVENTURE

This unusual vessel was the first warship laid down after the Great War, and was built at Devonport, completing on 5 May 1927. She had diesel-electric engines for cruising and could carry 340 mines. Pre-war she operated with the Home Fleet and then served on the China Station. In 1939 she laid a mine barrage in the Dover Straits and then carried out a lay off Flamborough Head. On 13 November 1939 she was damaged by a magnetic mine in the Thames Estuary, repairs taking 10 months. On 15 January 1941 she was severely damaged by an acoustic mine in Liverpool Bay. She was damaged by bombs whilst being repaired at Liverpool, and was not ready for further service until June 1941. She then took mines to Russia and depth charges and stores to the Mediterranean. On 10 April 1943 in the Bay of Biscay she intercepted a German blockade-runner, which scuttled herself. In February 1944 she was converted to an accommodation and maintenance ship and served at Normandy. She was broken up in 1947.

HMS CORNWALL (March 1931)

The next class of heavy cruiser built were limited by size and armament by International Treaties. The first group of this class were found to be under the designed displacement, and so provision was made for fitting them with aircraft and extra ammunition. CORNWALL was built at Devonport, being completed on 8 May 1928. In this view her high freeboard and the balanced layout of her four twin 8-inch turrets are clear. She served on the China Station until 1936, then refitted at Chatham with a hangar and twin 4-inch guns, but retained her high quarterdeck. She commissioned in March 1939, again for the China Station and in December 1939 operated in the South Atlantic. On 7 May 1941 she sank the German raider PINGUIN (HK33). In 1941 and 1942 she escorted troop convoys in the Indian Ocean. On 5 April 1942 she and her half sister DORSETSHIRE were together off Ceylon when they were attacked by 50 Japanese carrier borne aircraft. Both ships were quickly overwhelmed and sunk. She lost 190 of her crew.

HMS CUMBERLAND (8 April 1942)

CUMBERLAND was the first of the County class cruisers to complete. They were the first cruisers ordered after the Great War. These vessels proved good seaboats and were invaluable in their duties protecting merchant shipping in the wide oceans despite severe weather. CUMBERLAND was built by Vickers Armstrong and completed 23 January 1928. She served on the China Station until 1935, when she refitted with an aircraft hangar and a pair of twin 4-inch guns (later increased to two pairs). Her stern was cut down to compensate for the increase in weight. In 1936 she returned to the China Station. In December 1939 she was in the South Atlantic and took a supporting role in the Battle of the River Plate. She took part in the Dakar Expedition, was refitted in 1941 with tripod masts and extra AA equipment, undertook Arctic Convoys and in 1944 joined the Eastern Fleet, covering attacks on Sabang and Sumatra and in 1945 the assault on Rangoon.

HMS CUMBERLAND (1957)

Post war CUMBERLAND undertook trooping duties and in 1949-51 was stripped of most of her armament and used as a trials ship for new guns and other equipment. Her anti-torpedo bulges, which distinguished the first group of the County class, are clearly visible in this photograph. In this photograph she is seen with a prototype twin 6-inch gun for trials prior to installation in the Tiger class. She paid off in December 1958 and was broken up in 1959, and hence was both the first and the last of the County class in service.

HMS SUFFOLK

SUFFOLK was completed on 31 May 1928 at Portsmouth. She is seen here carrying out trials with the original design short funnels. Experience showed that the funnels needed extending by 15 feet to keep the bridge and gunnery controls clear of fumes. The 8-inch guns had an elevation of 70 degrees, and these ships could fire a 2048 pound broadside. She served on the China Station to 1935, and then was refitted with a hangar and four twin 4-inch guns, with her stern cut down in compensation for the extra weight.

HMS SUFFOLK (27 February 1940)

SUFFOLK joined the Home Fleet in late September 1939 having been fitted with one of the first operational radar sets. She escorted convoys and was in the Northern Patrol. In April she took a force to the Faeroes and later that month intercepted a German tanker. She bombarded Stavanger airport and afterwards came under heavy air attacks, returning with her stern under water. Repairs took until March 1941, when she rejoined the Home Fleet. In May she located and shadowed the BISMARCK using her radar. In August she escorted the first Russian convoy. She remained with the Home Fleet till December 1942, when she was refitted for the Eastern Fleet. In May 1944 she took part in the air strike on Sourabaya and in October bombarded the Nicobar Islands. In 1945 she escorted air strikes on Sumatra and covered the assault on Rangoon and bombarded Car Nicobar and Pt. Blair (Indian Ocean). In July 1945 she returned to the UK, was used on trooping tasks and then was placed in reserve before being broken up in 1948.

39

HMAS AUSTRALIA (1946)

AUSTRALIA was built on the Clyde and was completed on 24 April 1928. Her funnels were extended by 18 feet, 3 feet more than her Royal Naval sisters. She returned to Britain for the 1935 Jubilee Review of the Fleet and then served with the Mediterranean Fleet, returning to Australia in August 1936. In September 1940 she took part in the Dakar Operation. In March 1941 she returned to Australian waters and in July 1941 operated in the South Atlantic. From 1942-45 she served with US Forces in the South West Pacific and Australian waters. She was damaged in the action at Savo Island in August 1942. On 21 October 1944, off Leyte, she became the first Allied warship to be hit by a Kamikaze aircraft. Her Captain and 29 others were killed. She was also hit by 5 Kamikaze aircraft in Lingayen Gulf between 5 and 9 January 1945, losing 44 of her crew and being heavily damaged. She was repaired at Sydney and at Devonport, X-turret being removed. She was placed in reserve in 1946 but re-commissioned from 1951 to 1954. Such was the demand for steel in post-war Britain she was towed from Sydney on 26 March 1955 to Britain for breaking, a 101-day tow.

(MPL)

HMS KENT (31 March 1942)

KENT was launched at Chatham on 16 March 1926 and completed on 25 June 1928. After 8 years on the China Station, she underwent a long refit from 1937 to July 1938, but emerged, unlike her sisters, without an aircraft hangar. In 1940 she escorted convoys in the East Indies and then entered the Mediterranean, carrying out bombardments. In September was torpedoed by aircraft off Bardia (Libya). She had to be towed to Alexandria by the destroyer NUBIAN. She was repaired at Devonport, where she was damaged by bombing. She then escorted eighteen convoys to and from Russia and took parts in raids on the Norwegian coast. She paid off in 1945 and was sold for breaking in February 1948.

HMAS CANBERRA (1928)

CANBERRA, like her Australia sister AUSTRALIA, was built on the Clyde. She was launched on 31 May 1927 and completed on 10 July 1928. Like the AUSTRALIA she was fitted with very tall funnels, visible in this photograph. She served in Australian waters to 1940, when she was employed in the South Atlantic. In 1941 she escorted convoys and patrolled in the East Indies. In March 1941 she captured the German supply ships COBURG and KETTY BROVIG. In July 1942 she was part of the screen for the amphibious force operating in the Solomons. On the night 8/9 August a Japanese force attacked the Allied force off Savo island. CANBERRA was hit by at least 24 shells, all power failed and fires broke out. She had to be sunk by the USS SELFRIDGE. 84 of her crew were lost. She was replaced in the Australian Fleet by her half-sister SHROPSHIRE.
(MPL)

HMS LONDON (September 1947)

LONDON was the first of the second group of the County class cruisers. These ships had their anti-torpedo protection inside the hull, and their narrower hulls gave them a three-quarter knot speed advantage. Opportunity was also taken to site their bridges and funnels further aft to give a better arc of fire for the main armament. LONDON was built at Portsmouth and completed on 31 January 1929. She served in the Mediterranean from 1929-39, then underwent a major reconstruction, emerging with just two funnels and a new bridge structure similar to the Colony class. She served in home waters, in the Atlantic and with the Eastern Fleet. In June 1941 she intercepted three German supply vessels, which scuttled themselves. She also took part in Russian convoys. Post war she served in the Far East, and in April 1949 she was badly damaged by shore gunfire whilst trying to aid the AMETHYST in the River Yangtze. She paid off in September 1949 and arrived at Bo'ness to be broken up in January 1950.

(PRNM)

HMS DEVONSHIRE

DEVONSHIRE was completed at Devonport on 18 March 1929. Her pre-war service was mainly in the Mediterranean, with a short spell on the China Station 1932-33. She took part in the evacuation of Norway, being slightly damaged by near misses, and brought the King of Norway to Britain. She was in the Dakar operation and patrolled the South Atlantic for raiders and escorted convoys. In August 1940 she covered Russian convoys. In October 1941 she returned to the South Atlantic, sinking the German raider ATLANTIS on 22 November. In April 1942 she took part in the Madagascar operation and then served in the Eastern Fleet. In 1944 she rejoined the Home Fleet and covered operations on the Norwegian coast against TIRPITZ and other shipping. In May 1945 she took part in the occupation of Norway, and escorted the King of Norway back to Oslo. After a period of trooping duties, she was partly disarmed (as seen here) and was employed as the Cadets' Training Ship from May 1947 to September 1953. She was then placed in reserve and broken up in 1954.

HMS SUSSEX (1935)

SUSSEX was built by Hawthorn Leslie and completed on 19 March 1929. She then served on the Mediterranean Station, with a break from 1934-36 when she served on the Australian Station in an exchange with AUSTRALIA. These ships did not receive the same major pre-war modernisations as their earlier half sisters (apart from LONDON), but had 4 extra single 4-inch guns fitted. On 2 December 1939 she intercepted the German blockade-runner WATUSSI. In April 1940 she escorted troops to Harstad and in July was in collision in fog with the destroyer IMOGEN, which sank. On the night 17/18 September 1940 she was bombed whilst in dock at Greenock, and partly capsized. Repairs took until August 1942. She then served with the Home Fleet and later with the Eastern Fleet. On 26 February 1943 she sank the German tanker HOHENFRIEDBERG, and during operations in the East off Phuket Island shot down two Kamikaze aircraft. She remained in the Far East after the war, except for a refit at Devonport. She paid off at Portsmouth in February 1949 and in January 1950 arrived at Dalmuir to be broken up.

(MPL)

HMS SHROPSHIRE (28 April 1942)

SHROPSHIRE was completed by Beardmore on 12 September 1929. Much of her pre-war service was in the Mediterranean, where she was at the outbreak of war. In October she joined the S. Atlantic Station and in December intercepted a German ship. In February 1941 she carried out bombardments on Italian Somaliland. In March 1941 she intercepted a Vichy French ship. She joined the Home Fleet in July 1941 and escorted the carrier ARGUS to Russia. After a refit, she was handed over to the Royal Australian Navy to replace the lost CANBERRA in April 1943. This photograph shows war modifications, tripod masts, radar and enhanced AA armament. While with an American Task Force she covered landings at Leyte and in October 1944 attacked the Japanese battlefleet in Suriago Strait, obtaining several hits on a battleship. In January 1945, while at the Lingayen Gulf landings, she shot down several suicide aircraft. In June 1945 she assisted with the landings at Balikpapan and was at Sagami Bay for the formal surrender of Japan. She was laid up 1948 and was broken up in 1955.

HMS NORFOLK (8 March 1945)

NORFOLK was in the third group of the County class heavy cruisers. This class were fitted with an improved Mk II 8-inch gun and were better protected. She completed on 30 April 1930. Damaged by an air raid at Scapa Flow in March 1940, repairs took till July, when she rejoined the fleet and covered convoys to Iceland. In November she escorted convoys to the Cape. She covered the W. African area against raiders and in March covered a Halifax convoy. In May 1941 she and SUFFOLK sighted the German battleship BISMARCK in the Denmark Strait and shadowed her, and was present when she was sunk. In 1941 and 1942 she escorted Russian convoys. She was off the Azores for the N. African landings before returning to Russian convoys and relieving Spitzbergen. She was damaged during the action in December 1943 when the SCHARNHORST was sunk. In January 1945 she engaged an enemy convoy off Norway, sinking 2 merchant ships and 6 escorts. In June she escorted the King of Norway back to Oslo. She then sailed for the East Indies, and remained there until 1949 when she was placed in reserve. She was broken up in 1950.

HMS DORSETSHIRE

DORSETSHIRE was built by Portsmouth Dockyard and completed on 30 September 1930- note the stern-walk and aircraft amidships in this early photograph. She served in the Atlantic and on the Africa and China Stations before the war. In 1939 she operated in the Indian Ocean and S. Atlantic searching for raiders. In February 1940 she intercepted the German ship WAKAMA. She was in the Dakar Expedition in July 1940 and bombarded Somaliland in November 1940. In May 1941 she was detached from convoy duty to take part in the search for the German battleship BISMARCK, and steamed 600 miles to help sink the BISMARCK with torpedoes and gunfire, rescuing 80 survivors. In December 1941 she sank the German supply ship PYTHON in the South Atlantic. In April 1942 she was part of the Eastern Fleet off Ceylon. She and her half sister CORNWALL were attacked by Japanese carrier borne aircraft. Both ships were quickly overwhelmed and sunk.

HMS YORK

YORK was the first of a modified County class, distinguished by having two instead of three funnels. They also carried only three twin 8-inch guns. Completed at Jarrow on 1 May 1930, she had a high bridge to allow for a catapult on B gun, though it was never fitted. She served in the Atlantic and on the America and West Indies Station before the war. In March 1940 she intercepted the German ARUCAS off Iceland. She took part in the Norwegian campaign, landing and evacuating troops. She then sailed for the Mediterranean, covering convoys and supporting troops in Libya. In October 1940 she sank the damaged Italian destroyer ARTIGLIERE. She ferried troops to Greece, and on 26 March 1942 was damaged by an Italian explosive motor boat whilst in Suda Bay. Damaged in air attacks, she had to be abandoned on 22 May 1942. Her hull was broken up in 1952.

HMS EXETER

EXETER was built at Devonport Dockyard, completing in July 1931, the last RN heavy cruiser. She differed from her sister ship YORK in having vertical masts and funnels, and a new style bridge. She served in the Atlantic and America and West Indies Station before the war. When war broke out she sailed for the S. Atlantic to protect shipping and search for raiders. On 13 December 1939, she, and AJAX and ACHILLES, met and engaged the pocket battleship ADMIRAL GRAF SPEE. EXETER was severely mauled and had to retire to the Falklands. She was repaired at Devonport and sailed in March 1941 before completion due to the intensity of air raids. She escorted convoys in the Atlantic and Indian Ocean. In February 1942 she joined the Allied striking Force in the Java Sea. In the Battle of Java Sea, she was damaged by an enemy shell, which wrecked a boiler room. She sailed for Trincomalee, but on 1 March she and two destroyers encountered a vastly superior force of Japanese warships, and all 3 were sunk.

HMS LEANDER (16 October 1942)

LEANDER was one of the first class of light cruisers laid down after the Great War, and was a trial ship for the use of welding in her construction. They had a distinctive single funnel design. She was completed at Devonport on 24 March 1933 and served with the Home Fleet for 4 years before joining the New Zealand Division. When war began she was employed protecting trade routes in the Indian Ocean. In October 1940 she drove off Italian destroyers from a troop convoy, and in February 1941 she sank the Italian raider RAMB I. In June 1941, she damaged a French destroyer during the Syrian Campaign. She then returned to New Zealand and in 1942 joined the ANZAC Force. In July 1942, while intercepting Japanese destroyers carrying troops in the Solomons, she was torpedoed by a Japanese cruiser and badly damaged. Repairs were carried out at Auckland and then the USA - lasting to August 1945. During this time she was returned to the Royal Navy. She then joined the Mediterranean Fleet and was present at the Corfu incident on 22 October 1946. Paid off in early 1948, she was broken up in 1950 after use in trials.

(World Ship Photo Library)

HMS ACHILLES

ACHILLES came to public notice in December 1939, when she, AJAX and EXETER were in the action which led to the scuttling of the battleship ADMIRAL GRAF SPEE. During the action she was damaged by shell splinters. Afterwards she returned to New Zealand (as she was serving with the New Zealand Division of the Royal Navy) and then operated in the Indian Ocean until February 1942, when she joined with Australian and American forces operating off the New Hebrides. In January 1943 she moved to the SW Solomons. Whilst withdrawing from an operation her X turret was damaged by a bomb. She was repaired in the UK and in March 1944 joined the Eastern Fleet, and afterwards the newly formed British Pacific Fleet. In May 1945 she operated off the Sakishima-Gunto Group and later off Truk, and took part in attacks on the Tokyo and Yokohama area. She returned to the UK from New Zealand in 1946, in 1950 became the Indian Naval Ship DELHI and finally paid off in 1977.

HMS ORION

ORION was built at Devonport Dockyard, completing on 18 January 1934. In April 1940 she joined the Mediterranean Fleet. In June she and other cruisers encountered 3 Italian destroyers, HMAS SYDNEY sinking the Italian ESPERO. She was at the Battle of Matapan during which she came into action with the Italian battleship VITTORIO VENETO. She was severely damaged in the withdrawal from Crete in May 1941, losing over 100 crew and about 260 troops. After repairs she returned to the Mediterranean in September 1942, covering the first convoys to Malta from Egypt after the siege had been raised in November. She supported the landings in Sicily and Italy and then returned to UK to assist at Normandy. On completion, she returned to the Mediterranean for the landings in the South of France and for the operations leading to the re-entry into Greece. She left the Mediterranean finally in July 1946. This photograph shows her war modifications, twin 4-inch guns, tripod masts, radar and light AA guns. After use in explosive trials, she was broken up in 1949.

(David Scoble Collection)

53

HMS NEPTUNE

The cruiser NEPTUNE was completed by Portsmouth Dockyard in February 1934. She was on the S. Atlantic Station when war was declared. She immediately carried out searches, sinking the SS INN on 5 September 1939. She operated with hunting groups against raiders and enemy shipping until April 1940, when she joined the Mediterranean Fleet. In June 1940 she took part in bombardments and was in action with Italian destroyers on 28th, when one destroyer was sunk. In July she helped cover convoys to Malta and Alexandria and was at the action off Calabria, and also sank an enemy oil tanker. She escorted carriers taking aircraft to Malta. In August she returned to the S. Atlantic, intercepting an enemy tanker on 8 October. She returned to the Mediterranean via the Cape in June 1941, sinking a German tanker on passage. She helped reinforce troops in Cyprus and Tobruk and escorted convoys to Malta. On 19 December she ran onto mines off Libya, hitting four. She capsized and sank. There was only one survivor.

HMS AJAX

AJAX was built at Barrow being completed on 12 April 1935. She served on the America and West Indies Station, with a temporary detachment to the Mediterranean in 1935. On 13 December 1939 she took part in the Battle of the River Plate, flying off her aircraft for gunnery spotting. She is seen here returning to Chatham for repairs, with mainmast broken and X-turret damaged. Afterwards she sailed for the Mediterranean, where on 11/12 October 1940 she sank the Italian Torpedo Boats ARIEL and AIRONE and crippled the destroyer ARTIGLIERE off Malta. The next month she helped destroy an Italian convoy. She was at the Battle of Cape Matapan and assisted in the evacuation of Greece in April 1941 and of Crete the following month. She was badly damaged in an air attack at Bone in January 1943 and was repaired in the USA. She re-commissioned in December 1943 and served in the Mediterranean and at Normandy. Post war she served in S. American waters and the Mediterranean. She paid off in February 1948 and was broken up in 1949.

(Steve Bush Collection)

HMAS SYDNEY ex HMS PHAETON

PHAETON was built by Swan Hunter and completed on 24 September 1935, by which time she had been transferred to the Royal Australian Navy and had been renamed SYDNEY. This class were a repeat of the Leanders, but were given two separate boiler rooms (and funnels) to give a unit system which provided a better ability to cope with action damage. SYDNEY served in Australian waters to 1940, when she entered the Mediterranean, taking part in bombardments and convoy protection. In June 1940 she sank the Italian destroyer ESPERO and in July 1940 she and 5 destroyers engaged two Italian cruisers off Cape Spada. The BARTOLOMEO COLLEONI was hit and sunk. In January 1941 she returned to Australian waters. On 19 November 1941 she encountered the German raider KORMORAN off Shark Bay. During the action she was badly damaged and sank. All 645 on onboard were lost. The KORMORAN was also sunk.   (Royal Australian Navy)

HMS APOLLO, later HMAS HOBART

APOLLO was built at Devonport Dockyard, and was completed on 13 January 1936. This early photograph shows her four-turret layout and can be compared with the similar view of LEANDER on page 51. She served in the America and West Indies Station and returned to the UK to transfer to the Royal Australian Navy in 14 October 1938 as the HOBART. She served in the East Indies, Red Sea and Mediterranean before returning to Australia in 1941 for the Pacific. She was severely damaged off the New Hebrides on 20 July 1943 when hit by a torpedo from a Japanese submarine. She lost 13 dead. Repairs took until December 1944. She then worked up and joined the British Pacific Fleet. In 1953 she was taken in hand for conversion to a training ship, but was never completed. She was sold in March 1962, and was broken up in Japan.

HMS AMPHION, later HMAS PERTH   (August 1937)

AMPHION was built at Portsmouth, commissioning for trials in July 1936. She served on the African Station to December 1938. On 10 July 1939 she commissioned as HMAS PERTH, and sailed for Australia, with a spell in the Trinidad area to protect trade. She served in the Red Sea and in December 1940 joined the Mediterranean Fleet. She was at the Battle of Cape Matapan in March 1941. In May 1941 she was at Crete, coming under heavy air attack and used over 1,000 rounds of 4-inch and 2700 rounds of 2-pounder ammunition. Fortunately she had a pompom in place of her catapult. She was damaged by bombs on 22 and 30 May 1941, south of Crete. In July 1941 she returned to Sydney to refit. In January 1942 she joined the ABDA force (American, British, Dutch, Australian) in the Java Sea and took part in the action against Japanese invasion forces on 27 February 1942. On the night 28 February/1 March 1942, she, and US cruiser HOUSTON, encountered Japanese invasion Forces at the Sunda Strait, and both ships were lost in the ensuing action. 353 of her crew died in the action, and a further 105 died in captivity.

(MPL)

HMS ARETHUSA (November 1945)

ARETHUSA was the first of a new class of light cruiser, designed to work with destroyers rather than protect trade. Armed with three twin 6-inch guns, she had a speed of 32.25 knots. These ships were lightly armoured and welding was used in their construction to save weight. She completed on 23 May 1935. Pre-war she served in the Mediterranean. She left the Mediterranean in October 1939 and took part in operations off Norway, where she was damaged in air attacks. She returned to the Mediterranean in August 1941 and helped escort convoys to Malta. After a refit she returned to the Mediterranean in May 1942 and took part in Operation Vigorous, a vain attempt to run a convoy to Malta from the East. In November 1942 she escorted another convoy to Malta, during which she was torpedoed and badly damaged, losing 156 dead. All 4 merchant ships of the convoy reached Malta safely and relieved the siege. After repairs in the USA, she took part in the Normandy landings, carrying King George VI to the beaches. She was mined there later. She returned to the Mediterranean from January to November 1945, when she paid off. She was broken up in 1950 after being used in target trials. (PRNM)

HMS GALATEA

GALATEA was completed at Greenock on 14 August 1935. The first 2 ships of the class carried just four single 4-inch AA guns amidships, as can be seen here. The later 2 ships had twin mountings fitted and the first 2 were retrofitted later. Pre-war she served in the Mediterranean. In March 1940 she joined the Home Fleet and carried out sweeps of the Skagerrik. During the Norwegian campaign she was bombed several times but not damaged. In May she bombarded Calais and covered the evacuation of Dunkirk. She was mined in September and repairs took till January 1941 to complete. She then rejoined the Home Fleet, carrying out sweeps, patrols and covering minelaying operations. In August 1941 she returned to the Mediterranean via the Cape. She supported the relief of Tobruk in August and the next month operated in the Red Sea. She carried out bombardments near Tobruk in October. She was returning from an operation in the Central Mediterranean on 14 December 1941 when she was torpedoed and sunk by U-557, with the loss of 470 of her crew.

HMS PENELOPE

PENELOPE was built at Belfast and completed on 13 November 1936. Her twin 4-inch guns can been seen amidships.in this photograph taken on her trials. The AA director on her bridge and the other abaft her mainmast had not been fitted when photographed. She served in the Mediterranean before the war. She was damaged by grounding in the Norwegian campaign, repairs taking until August 1941 to complete. She then returned to the Mediterranean as part of the very successful Force K, operating out of Malta against Italian convoys to N. Africa. She took part in the Second Battle of Sirte in March 1942, fighting a convoy through to Malta. She came under intensive bombing whilst in harbour at Malta, firing 6,500 rounds of 4-inch and 75,000 rounds of smaller ammunition in 10 days. The splinter damage she received earning her the name 'Pepperpot'. After repairs she returned to the Mediterranean, taking part in the landings at Salerno and Anzio. In February 1944 she was torpedoed by U-410 off the Anzio beachhead and sank in 10 minutes. (MPL)

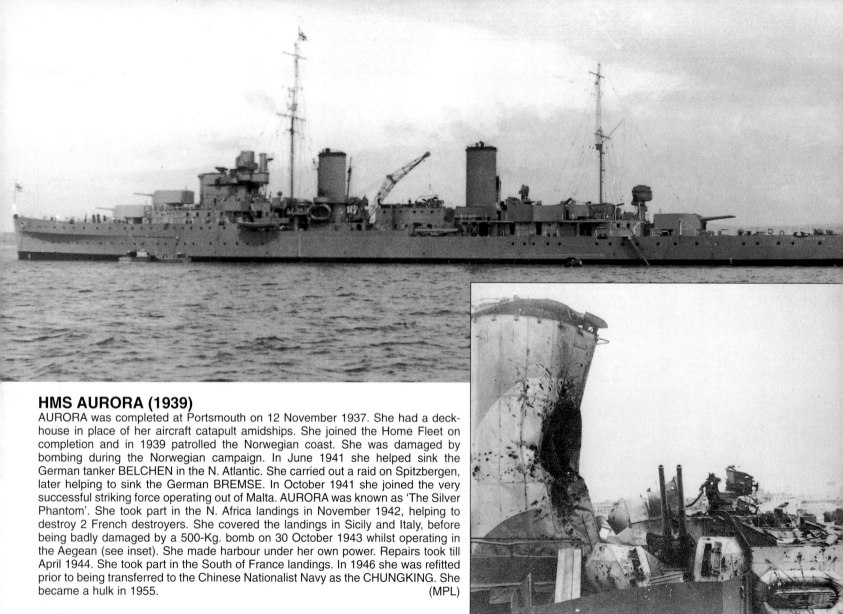

HMS AURORA (1939)

AURORA was completed at Portsmouth on 12 November 1937. She had a deck-house in place of her aircraft catapult amidships. She joined the Home Fleet on completion and in 1939 patrolled the Norwegian coast. She was damaged by bombing during the Norwegian campaign. In June 1941 she helped sink the German tanker BELCHEN in the N. Atlantic. She carried out a raid on Spitzbergen, later helping to sink the German BREMSE. In October 1941 she joined the very successful striking force operating out of Malta. AURORA was known as 'The Silver Phantom'. She took part in the N. Africa landings in November 1942, helping to destroy 2 French destroyers. She covered the landings in Sicily and Italy, before being badly damaged by a 500-Kg. bomb on 30 October 1943 whilst operating in the Aegean (see inset). She made harbour under her own power. Repairs took till April 1944. She took part in the South of France landings. In 1946 she was refitted prior to being transferred to the Chinese Nationalist Navy as the CHUNGKING. She became a hulk in 1955. (MPL)

HMS NEWCASTLE (February 1946)

NEWCASTLE was the first of the Southampton class to complete on 5 March 1937. This class were limited in displacement by International Treaties, and there was criticism of their capabilities when compared to contemporary cruisers in other navies, the American and Japanese cruisers carrying 15 6-inch guns. They were, however, handsome ships with a balanced gunnery armament of four triple 6-inch guns backed by an AA armament of four twin 4-inch and pom-poms. NEWCASTLE served in the Home Fleet in the North Sea and protected convoys. In September 1940 she joined Force H at Gibraltar and took part in an engagement with the Italian Fleet. She operated in the S. Atlantic and with the Eastern Fleet and in June 1943 entered the Mediterranean to help escort a convoy to Malta. During this she was torpedoed by an E-boat, and was repaired at Bombay and New York. In March 1944 she rejoined the Eastern Fleet, covering raids on Sabang, Sourabaya and Akyab. In May 1945 she was refitted on the Tyne, her X turret being removed. She was again refitted in 1950-52 with a lattice foremast and was at Korea 1952-53. She bombarded guerrilla positions in Malaya in 1954-55. She paid off in 1958 and was broken up in 1959.   (MPL)

HMS SOUTHAMPTON

SOUTHAMPTON was the name ship of her class. She was built on the Clyde and completed on 6 March 1937. Her pre-war appearance can be compared with views of sister ships modernised later. These ships had a speed of 32 knots, and most exceeded this on trials. At the outbreak of war she was with the Home Fleet. She was bombed at Rosyth on 16 October 1939. After duty on the Northern Patrol, she took part in the Norwegian campaign, coming under air attack and being damaged three times in April and May. She took part in the final evacuation of Norway in June 1940. She transferred to the Mediterranean and was at the action off Cape Spartivento in November1940. Later that month she escorted troop convoys in the Indian Ocean, returning to the Mediterranean on 1 January 1941. With BONAVENTURE she sank the Italian torpedo boat VEGA off Pantellaria on 10 January 1941. The next day she came under heavy air attack, was damaged and caught fire. The fires became uncontrollable and she had to be abandoned. 81 of her crew died and 87 were wounded.

HMS SHEFFIELD (1957)

The SHEFFIELD was built on the Tyne and completed on 25 August 1937. This third, and subsequent ships of this class had an extra AA director aft. She was fitted with air warning radar before the war. She took part in the action against the BISMARCK in May 1941. She forced the German tanker FRIEDRICH BREME to scuttle on 12 June 1941. In March 1942 she was damaged by a mine. She took part in Russian convoys, during which she helped beat off a German heavy cruiser, pocket battleship and destroyers whilst defending a convoy on 31 December 1942. In that action she sank the German destroyer FRIEDRICH ECKHOLDT. She took part in the action when the German battlecruiser SCHARNHORST was sunk in December 1943. She refitted in the USA from July 1944 to May 1945. Post war she served in the West Indies and later was refitted with a new bridge and foremast (as can be seen here). She paid off in January 1959 and was towed to Rosyth to de-equip in January 1967 prior to being broken up at Faslane in September 1967. (World Ship Photo Library)

HMS BIRMINGHAM

BIRMINGHAM was built at Devonport and completed on 18 November 1937. Her extra AA director aft is clearly visible in this wartime photograph, which also shows her extra small AA guns and radar equipment. She was on the China Station to January 1940 then joined the Home Fleet, serving in the Norwegian campaign. In June 1941 she joined the S. Atlantic Station until February 1942. In June 1942 she took part in Operation Vigorous, an unsuccessful convoy to Malta. She was slightly damaged by a torpedo during that operation. She rejoined the Eastern Fleet in July 1942 and in September 1942 took part in the invasion of Madagscar. She then carried out trade protection patrols in the Indian Ocean. After a refit in the UK she returned to the Mediterranean on 28 November 1943. Whilst on passage to the East she was torpedoed off Cyrenaica by U-407. Repairs in the USA took until November 1944. She remained with the Home Fleet and after a refit served in the East Indies.

(Dave Scoble Collection)

HMS BIRMINGHAM

BIRMINGHAM was reconstructed at Portsmouth 1950-52 and fitted with a lattice foremast, new bridge, new AA fire control systems and tertiary armament. This view shows her distinctive bow, which was without the usual cruiser knuckle. She served in the Far East and took part in the Korean War from September 1952 until it ended in July 1953. She later served in the Mediterranean and home waters. She paid off in 1959 and was broken up in 1960.

HMS GLASGOW (1943)

GLASGOW was built at Greenock and completed on 9 September 1937. She achieved 32.8 knots on trials. She was with the Home Fleet when war was declared. During the Norwegian campaign she landed seamen and Royal Marines, was damaged in air attacks, helped evacuate Aandalsnes, and took the King of Norway to Tromso. On 17 July 1940 she collided with the destroyer IMOGEN, which exploded and sank. In November she escorted convoys to Malta. In December 1940 she was hit by two aircraft launched torpedoes while at Crete, but was able to reach Alexandria under her own power. After temporary repairs she operated in the Indian Ocean and in May 1942 she sailed for a refit at New York, which lasted till August. In March 1943 she intercepted the blockade-runner REGENSBURG. In December she and ENTERPRISE engaged 11 German destroyers and torpedo boats, sinking three. During the Normandy landings she was hit by shore batteries. After repairs she sailed for the Far East, arriving at Colombo after VJ Day. She finally paid off in 1956 and was handed over for breaking up in 1958.   (Eric Abrams Collection)

HMS MANCHESTER (AUGUST 1938)

MANCHESTER was one of three slightly improved versions of the Southampton class, fitted with a Flag bridge and improved main armament. The extra 6-inch director aft can be seen in this photograph. She completed on 4 August 1938 and was allocated to the East Indies Fleet, where she was on station when war was declared. In spring 1940 she was part of the Northern Patrol and during the Norwegian campaign took part in the expedition to Namsos. In November she returned to the Mediterranean to escort convoys. She refitted in UK in spring 1941, and took part in the search for the BISMARCK. After more patrols in the North, she was an escort to the Substance convoy to Malta in July 1941, during which she was hit by an aircraft launched torpedo. She was repaired in the USA. In June 1942 she helped cover Russian convoys and to relieve Spitzbergen. In August 1942 she again went south to escort the Pedestal convoy to Malta. At midnight 12/13 August she was torpedoed by Motor Torpedo Boats off Cape Bon. Disabled, she had to be scuttled. (PRNM)

HMS LIVERPOOL (June 1951)

LIVERPOOL was built by Fairfield and completed on 25 October 1938. She was on the East Indies Station at the outbreak of war, protecting trade routes. In November she operated off Japan, and in April 1940 was in the Red Sea. In May 1940 she transferred to the Mediterranean, and the next month was in action with Italian destroyers, of which one was sunk. She took part in the action off Calabria and on 29 July was bombed whilst escorting a convoy in the Aegean. She then escorted convoys and carried troops to Malta. While returning from an operation covering air attacks on Leros (Greece), she was torpedoed forward, and her bows were wrecked and broke off and sank. Repairs in the USA took till January 1942. She then took part in Russian convoys. On 14 June 1942 she was escorting a convoy to Malta. LIVERPOOL was a prime target for air attacks, and was torpedoed and badly damaged. She was taken in tow for Gibraltar, and arrived safely despite further attacks. Repairs took till July 1945. In October 1945 she rejoined the Mediterranean Fleet. She paid off in 1952 and was broken up in 1958.   (MPL)

HMS GLOUCESTER (13 March 1940)

GLOUCESTER was completed in Devonport Dockyard on 31 January 1939 and sailed for the East Indies just before the war started. She carried out patrols off East Africa and in the Indian Ocean and returned to the Mediterranean in May 1940. She was damaged by bombs during sweeps of the Eastern Mediterranean, her bridge was hit but she continued to operate steering from her after control position. In September 1940 she helped convoy troops to Malta and in November escorted the ILLUSTRIOUS when her aircraft attacked Taranto. In March 1941 she took part in the Battle of Matapan. During the evacuation of Crete she and the FIJI remained close to shore to cover destroyers recovering survivors from another destroyer. However, both cruisers were by then low on AA ammunition and came under heavy air attacks. Both cruisers were sunk. GLOUCESTER lost 724 of her crew, only 83 surviving.   (MPL)

HMS EDINBURGH (October 1941)

EDINBURGH was completed by Swan Hunter on 6 July 1939. The two ships of this class (her sister was BELFAST) were armed with four triple 6-inch turrets, and were 22 feet longer and beamier than the Southamptons. They carried an extra pair of twin 4-inch AA guns and were distinguished by their unusual funnel layout, clearly visible in this photograph. When the war began she was used on patrols between Iceland and the Faeroes, and then transferred to the Humber Force. She suffered minor damage from a near miss during air attacks in the Firth of Forth in October 1939. She covered convoys and the raid on the Lofoten Islands in March 1941. She also carried out patrols in the Denmark Strait. She entered the Mediterranean to cover the convoys to Malta in July 41 (Substance) and September 41.

(IWM Neg No: A6160)

HMS EDINBURGH

In December 1941 EDINBURGH escorted Russian convoys, and on 30 April 1942, whilst covering return convoy QP11her stern was blown off by torpedoes fired by U-456. This photo shows the damage to her after section. She was taken in tow bound for Murmansk, but later managed to proceed slowly under her own power. On 2 May she came under air attack, and then encountered 3 German destroyers, one of which she hit and disabled. She was again torpedoed, and had to be abandoned and sunk. 58 of her crew were lost. Gold bullion she was carrying was recovered in 1981.

HMS BELFAST (October 1948)

BELFAST was built at Belfast and was completed on 3 August 1939 and immediately joined the Home Fleet. On 21 November 1939 she was mined in the Firth of Forth, and repairs to her broken back took 3 years. She rejoined the Fleet in December 1942, virtually a new ship. The extra strengthening fitted to her hull is clearly visible in this scene. She then joined the Home Fleet to cover convoys to Northern Russia. In December 1943 it was her radar that detected the German battlecruiser SCHARNHORST and allowed the British forces to close and sink the enemy. She also supported operations against the TIRPITZ. She took part in bombardments with the Eastern Task Force at Normandy. In July 1944 she was refitted and in June 1945 sailed for the Far East, but did not arrive until after the Japanese surrender. She returned to the UK in 1947. She took part in the Korean War from July 1950, carrying out bombardments and blockades, firing over 8,000 rounds of 6-inch and covering 82,500 miles.

(MPL)

HMS BELFAST

BELFAST left the Korean Theatre in September 1952 and returned to the UK to be placed in reserve. She was modernised at Devonport from 1956-59. She emerged with lattice masts, new bridgework and improved AA systems. Unlike other light cruisers, she was large enough to retain her fourth triple 6-inch turret despite the extra equipment added throughout her career. She again served in the Far East. She was placed in reserve in 1965. In November 1971 she was towed to the Thames and opened to the public.

HMS BONAVENTURE (October 1940)

BONAVENTURE was lead ship of the Dido class of light cruisers, being completed at Greenock on 24 May 1940. These ships were small, intended for rapid production and were armed with five twin 5.25-inch guns, giving them a good AA capability. With a speed of 32.25 knots, these were handy vessels, but carried a lot of topweight, which limited any later additions. BONAVENTURE was completed without X turret due to supply problems. On 25 December 1940, whilst escorting a convoy, she helped drive off the German heavy cruiser ADMIRAL HIPPER, firing 400 rounds of 5.25-inch. On 28 December 1940 she intercepted the German SS BADEN and sank her by torpedo. In January 1941 she entered the Mediterranean and on 10 January with the SOUTHAMPTON sank the Italian torpedo boat VEGA. She took part in convoy operations, coming under heavy air attacks. On 31 March 1941, whilst escorting a convoy, she was hit by two torpedoes from the Italian submarine AMBRA South east of Crete and sank with the loss of 138 of her crew.

HMS NAIAD (May 1941)

NAIAD was the second of the Dido class to complete (on 24 July 1940), being built by Hawthorn Leslie. She was equipped with all five turrets. After patrols with the Home Fleet, which included a raid on Jan Mayen Island and sighting the SCHARNHORST and GNEISENAU, in April 1941 she took a convoy to the Mediterranean whilst on passage to join the Mediterranean Fleet. She took part in the Battle of Crete in May, attacking sea-borne invasion craft. During a two-hour air attack, 181 bombs were aimed at her. Two of her turrets were put out of action. She also escorted convoys to Malta. She also supported land operations in Syria and the Western Desert. In December 1941 she fired 200 rounds during a bombardment of Derna. In February 1942 she was with a convoy to Malta that came under intense air attack and had to retire. She was the Flagship of Admiral Vian in March 1942, when she was on an operation to intercept convoys between Italy and Libya and meet reinforcements. On 11th, when South of Crete, she was torpedoed amidships by U-565. She sank in 35 minutes, 591of her crew being rescued.

(IWM Neg No: A447)

HMS DIDO

DIDO, name ship for the class, was built at Birkenhead and completed on 30 September 1940. Due to shortages, she was commissioned with a 4-inch gun in Q position instead of a twin 5.25-inch turret. This view shows her with the fifth mounting, fitted in 1941, and also shows the high elevation of these guns. DIDO joined the Home Fleet and carried out blockade operations and escort duties. She joined the Mediterranean Fleet in April 1941, taking part in the evacuation of Greece. In the battle for Crete she helped sink a German invasion convoy and during the evacuation she was bombed, with heavy casualties among the troops onboard. After repairs in Brooklyn she returned to the Mediterranean. Whilst escorting a convoy to Malta she and 3 other light cruisers and destroyers drove off an Italian battleship and heavy cruisers. She also carried out bombardments and operated against enemy shipping. She took part in landings in Sicily and Italy. Later she covered convoys to Russia and attacks on the Norwegian coast. In May 1945 she helped take the surrender of Copenhagen. She was placed in reserve in 1947 and eventually broken up in 1958.

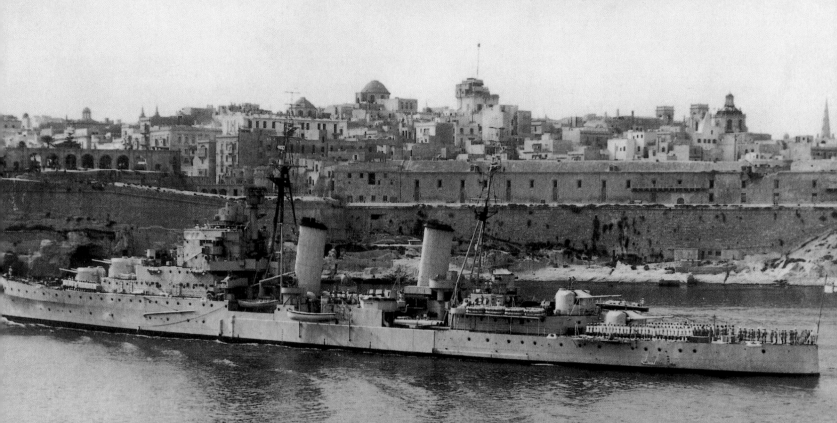

HMS PHOEBE (October 1948)

PHOEBE was built by Fairfield and completed on 30 September 1940. She was completed without Q turret, which was never installed. After convoy escort duties with the Home Fleet, she joined the Mediterranean Fleet. She took part in the evacuation of Crete in May 1941 and in August 1941 was damaged by aircraft attack and was repaired in the USA. She was operational by July 1942 and the next month escorted a convoy to Malta (Operation Pedestal). Afterwards she sailed for the S. Atlantic and was torpedoed off French Equatorial Africa in October 1942, and again was repaired in the USA. In September 1943 she rejoined the Mediterranean Fleet. She took part in operations in the Aegean and at Anzio. In May 1944 she transferred to the Eastern Fleet and helped cover attacks on the Andamans, Sabang and the Nicobars. In January 1945 she took part in the capture of the Akyab and Ramree Island, and in May 1945 was at the assault on Rangoon. In October 1945 she returned to UK and after a refit joined the Mediterranean Fleet in June 1946, where she remained until March 1951. She then paid off and was broken up in March 1956.

HMS HERMIONE

HERMIONE was completed at Glasgow on 25 March 1941. She carried all five twin 5.25-inch guns and was desperately needed by a Fleet short of anti-aircraft capability. After operating with the Home Fleet she joined Force H, based on Gibraltar, in June 1941. She took part in the July (Substance) convoy to Malta. Shortly afterwards she carried troops to Malta, and during the operation she rammed and sank the Italian submarine TEMBIEN. In October and November she covered operations to ferry aircraft to Malta. During the second of these operations, the carrier ARK ROYAL was lost. In March 1942 she took part in further aircraft ferrying operations. In April she sailed south for the Madagascar operation. In June she joined the Mediterranean Fleet at Alexandria. On 13 June she sailed on Operation Vigorous. HERMIONE helped beat off heavy air attacks, but the convoy had to turn back. During the return passage to Alexandria, on 16 June 1942, she was torpedoed by U-205 South of Crete and sank in 21 minutes with the loss of 87 of her crew.

HMS EURYALUS (9 October 1941)

EURYALUS was built at Chatham and completed on 30 June 1941. She escorted a convoy to Malta in September 1941 before joining the Mediterranean Fleet via the Cape. She carried out bombardments and escorted troopships. She also escorted convoys to Malta, taking part in the Second Battle of Sirte in March 1942, when she and other light cruisers and destroyers drove off an Italian battleship and heavy cruisers from a convoy. In November she escorted the first convoy to Malta after the siege had been raised. After supporting landings in Sicily and Salerno, she returned to the UK for a refit in October 1943, having not sustained any damage despite being in the fiercest fighting. After operations off the Norwegian coast, she sailed for operations against Japan, covering strikes against Sumatra before joining the British Pacific Fleet. She took part in operations against the Ryukyu Islands (SW of Japan) and the mainland of Japan. She was at the relief of Hong Kong in August 1945. She returned to the UK in 1947, and was placed in reserve in 1954. She was broken up in 1959.

HMS SIRIUS (November 1944)

SIRIUS was built at Portsmouth Dockyard and completed on 6 May 1942 after delays caused by bombing. She was completed with all five turrets, retaining them throughout her career, though other ships had their Q turret replaced by light AA guns to provide defence from attacks over the bow. She immediately joined the Home Fleet and operated in support of Russian convoys. In August 1942 she helped escort the Pedestal convoy to Malta, which came under heavy attacks and only 5 out of 14 merchant ships reached the island. She then operated in the South Atlantic on patrols and in November 1942 covered the N. African landings before joining a striking force operating out of Bone. Whilst with this force, she helped sink an enemy convoy of 4 ships together with an escorting destroyer.

(IWM Neg No: A27432)

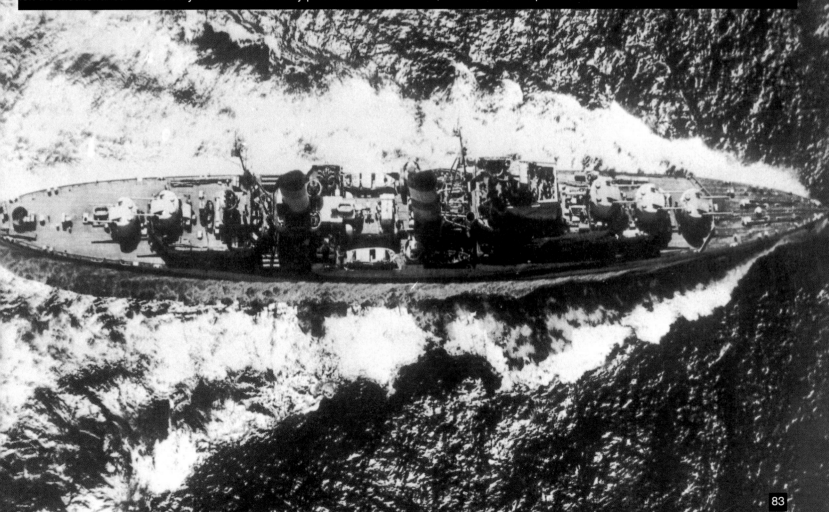

HMS SIRIUS (6 July 1942)

This overhead view of SIRIUS at speed shows the fine lines of these beautiful ships. The quadruple 2-pounders and torpedo tubes port and starboard of the aft funnel are clear in this photograph. In July 1943 she was part of the covering force for the Sicilian landings, and carried out bombardments both on Sicily and on the Italian mainland. In September she carried troops to Taranto (Italy). In October she transferred to the Levant and helped destroy an enemy convoy on 7th. Later that month she was bombed and repairs took 4 months. She took part in the Normandy landings, then returned to the Mediterranean for the South of France landings and in September 1944 entered Toulon. She helped in the re-occupation of Athens in October 1944. She left the Mediterranean in February 1946 and was finally placed in reserve in 1949, and was broken up in 1956.

HMS CLEOPATRA (1941)

CLEOPATRA was built by Hawthorn Leslie and completed on 20 November 1941. She joined the Mediterranean Fleet in February 1942 and was damaged by a bomb at Malta. She was one of the 4 cruisers that drove off an Italian battleship and heavy cruisers from a convoy to Malta in March 1942. She took part in the unsuccessful Vigorous convoy to Malta in June 1942, and escorted the Stoneage convoy that relieved Malta in November 1942. She was at the Sicilian landings in July 1943 and on 16 July 1943 was torpedoed by the Italian submarine DANDOLO. She was repaired at Philadelphia (when Q turret was removed and she was fitted with US close range guns) and then the Clyde until March 1945. She then returned to the Mediterranean, and served in the East Indies, being in the first group of British ships to enter Singapore in September 1945. In January 1946 she returned to the Home Fleet. She was at the Coronation Review in 1953, and that October was laid up at Chatham. She was broken up in December 1958 at Newport.   (Steve Bush Collection)

HMS ARGONAUT

ARGONAUT was built at Birkenhead, completing on 8 August 1942. She, and five other ships of the class, had been delayed by shortages, and she was the only one to complete to the original design. Her Q turret was replaced by a quadruple 2-pounder in 1944. In October 1942 she carried out a special trip to North Russia taking aid for British sick and wounded there, returning with survivors from earlier convoys. She then sailed south for the North African landings. Whilst returning from a sweep as part of a striking force based on Bone she was torpedoed at 25 knots by the Italian Submarine MOCENIGO, losing her bow and stern. She was still able to proceed slowly and help fight off air attacks. After temporary repairs she crossed the Atlantic to Philadelphia, steering by main engines. Her repairs there and later in the UK lasted to March 1944. She took part in the Normandy landings, firing 4395 shells in 25 days. In August 1944 she took part in the landings in the South of France, and then operated in the Aegean. Afterwards she joined the East Indies Fleet for strikes on Sumatra and went on to join the British Pacific Fleet, taking part in the operations off Okinawa. She returned to the UK in June 1946, being placed in reserve and then broken up in 1955.

HMS CHARYBDIS

Production difficulties arose with the 5.25-inch gun and two Didos, SCYLLA and CHARYBDIS, were completed with four twin 4.5-inch gun instead. Built by Cammell Laird, CHARYBDIS completed on 3 December 1941. After trials and work up she joined the Home Fleet, covering minelaying operations. In 1942 she covered reinforcements for Malta. In the autumn she operated in the North Atlantic searching for blockade-runners and in October again covered aircraft reinforcements for Malta. In November 1942 she joined Force H and carried the Allied Force HQ for Operation Torch to Algiers. Next month she rejoined the Home Fleet and patrolled the North Sea, covering minelaying operations and convoys in the Bay of Biscay. In August 1943 she escorted convoys in the Mediterranean and took part in the Salerno landings. She returned to the Bay of Biscay patrols. On 23 October 1943 she was torpedoed off the Channel Islands by German destroyers and was lost with 462 lives.

HMS SCYLLA (August 1943)

The SCYLLA was the other Dido class cruiser completed with 4.5-inch guns instead of 5.25-inch. This view shows her 4.5-inch guns. She completed at Greenock on 12 June 1942 and immediately took part in convoy PQ18 to Russia, where her AA capabilities were tested and proved. She took part in the North African landings and sank the blockade-runner RHAKOTIS in December 1942. In January 1943 she was refitted and took part in further convoys to Russia. In August 1943 she operated in the Bay of Biscay where she was damaged by a near miss during an air attack. She then returned to the Mediterranean to support the landings at Salerno. She returned to UK for repairs, and was part of the Task Force for the Normandy landings, acting as Flagship and carrying out bombardments. She was damaged on 14 June when a mine blew up nearby. She was able to limp to Spithead and then paid off at Chatham. Never repaired, she was laid up and broken up in 1950.   (Dave Scoble Collection)

HMS SPARTAN

The last five Dido class cruisers were completed to a modified design, with a lower silhouette and without Q turret. Light AA guns were fitted ahead of the bridge to provide cover from bow attacks after experience gained in PHOEBE in 1942. SPARTAN was built at Barrow, being launched 27 August 1942 and completed 10 August 1943. She was allocated to the Eastern Fleet but was retained in home waters and detached temporarily to the Mediterranean in October 1943. On 18 January 1944 she carried out a bombardment off Italy, firing 900 rounds of main armament. She supported the landings at Anzio on 22 January, and on 29 January, whilst still off the beaches, was hit by a glider bomb. She lost steam and electrical power, a fire developed and she had to be abandoned. She sank after 70 minutes with the loss of 46 of her crew.

HMS BELLONA (1952)

BELLONA was built by Fairfield and completed on 29 October 1943. These ships were easily distinguished from the earlier Didos by the lack of rake to their masts and funnels. BELLONA served with the Home Fleet, operating in the Western Channel against enemy shipping, and was a reserve bombardment ship for the Normandy landings. She then operated off the Norwegian Coast and also in the Bay of Biscay. On 6 August 1944 she severely damaged an enemy convoy and its escort off St. Nazaire, sinking several ships. After further bombardments, she returned to the Norwegian Coast where she damaged an enemy convoy on 12 November 1944. She escorted convoys to Russia and continued to operate off the Norwegian Coast until the war ended. She served in the Royal New Zealand Navy from 1946, returning to the UK in 1952 for Exercise Mainbrace. She was returned to the Royal Navy in 1956 and replaced IN THE RNZN by the ROYALIST. Laid up at Devonport, she was towed away for breaking up on 5 February 1959.

(PRNM)

HMS BLACK PRINCE

BLACK PRINCE was built at Belfast and completed on 20 November 1943. She operated against blockade-runners in the Bay of Biscay and in February 1944 took part in Arctic convoys. In April 1944 she was in action with German destroyers in the Channel, one destroyer being sunk. During the Normandy landings she was with the Western (US) Task Force, coming under fire from ashore. In August 1944 she took part in the landings in the South of France and then served in the Aegean carrying out bombardments and in operations against enemy shipping. In October 1944 she was at Athens helping to restore law and order and then operated with the East Indies Fleet against Sumatra. She joined the British Pacific Fleet in March 1945 and took part in Operations off Okinawa and then the Sakishima-Gunto Group. In July she shelled the Hitachi area of Honshu (Japan). She was lent to the Royal New Zealand Navy in 1946 and was at the Coronation Review in 1953. Paid off in 1960, she was broken up in 1962.

HMS ROYALIST (1959)

ROYALIST was built at Greenock and completed on 10 September 1943. She served with the Home Fleet and in the Arctic to June 1944. In August 1944 she was in the Mediterranean for the South of France landings and on 15 September 1944, with the destroyer TEAZER, sank two German vessels in the Aegean. In May 1945 she assisted in the capture of Rangoon and in August /September was at the surrender of Japanese forces in the East Indies. She returned to the UK in January 1946 and was placed in reserve, being part of the Torpedo School at Portsmouth in 1947-49. In 1955 she was brought forward for a major refit, involving a new bridge, gunnery control systems, secondary armament and lattice masts (as seen in this view). She was transferred to the Royal New Zealand Navy from 1956. In 1957 and 1958 she operated against terrorists in Malaya. She was returned to RN control in 1967. She was broken up in Japan in 1968.

(Vic Jeffery Collection)

HMS DIADEM (December 1945)

DIADEM was built by Hawthorn Leslie and completed on 6 January 1944, being the last of the British small cruisers to be built. She joined the Home Fleet, covered convoys to Russia, was a bombarding ship at Normandy and carried out patrols in the Bay of Biscay in July to September 1944. She also took part in anti-shipping operations off the Norwegian coast 1944-45. On 28 January 1945 she and the MAURITIUS intercepted 3 German destroyers off Bergen. Two of the destroyers were set on fire and both cruisers were damaged by shell-fire. In March 1945 she escorted convoys to Russia and in May operated off the Norwegian coast. She arrived at Copenhagen on 23 May 1945 and was at Oslo and Bergen in June 1945 to support the return to home rule. She was placed in reserve at Chatham in 1950 and on 29 February 1956 was sold to Pakistan, being commissioned as the BABUR in July 1957 after a refit. She was renamed JAHANGIR in 1982, used for harbour training and deleted in 1985, the last of her class.

(PRNM)

HMS NIGERIA
Built on the Tyne, NIGERIA was completed on 23 September 1940. The Colony class vessels were (again) limited in size by Treaty, and efforts were made to compress the Southamptons' capability into a smaller hull by re-designing the after boiler room and fitting a transom stern. In 1941 NIGERIA took part in an early commando raid in the Lofotens; the capture of German cypher equipment; sinking the German minelaying BREMEN; and escorting Russian convoys. She took part in a Malta convoy (Pedestal), which came under severe air attack and during which she was torpedoed by an Italian submarine. She was forced to limp back to Gibraltar. Repaired in the USA, she operated off Norway before joining the Eastern Fleet where she operated in the Indian Ocean, covering air attacks on Sumatra and the Andamans and bombarded Sabang in July 1944. She covered the Akyab landings in January 1945 and returned to UK in November 1945. By the end of the war only she and the GAMBIA of the Colony class retained X turret. She then served in the Mediterranean and South Atlantic before paying off in 1950. She was purchased by the Indian Navy in 1954, and after a major refit commissioned as MYSORE in 1957. She was deleted in 1986.

(PRNM)

HMS FIJI (1941)

This is one of the few photographs of FIJI, the first of the Colony class cruisers. She was launched on the Clyde on 31 May 1939 and completed on 17 May 1940. The class were distinguished by their narrow, vertical funnels and lack of rake to their masts. In August 1940 FIJI set out on the Dakar Expedition, but was torpedoed 40 miles off Rockall. Repairs took to March 1941. She then undertook patrols off Iceland and covered convoys. She transferred to the Mediterranean Fleet and took part in operations off Crete in May. She landed troops and carried out sweeps to prevent German landings. On 22 May she and GLOUCESTER closed the coast of Crete to cover two destroyers rescuing survivors. They came under heavy air attacks. FIJI survived 20 attacks in four hours but was hit by a single bomb from an aircraft that came out of cloud cover. She was badly damaged, and then hit by three more bombs from another single aircraft. She sank but over 500 of her crew were rescued. (MPL)

HMS KENYA (April 1958)

KENYA was completed on 27 September 1940 and joined the Home Fleet. She screened the carrier VICTORIOUS during the BISMARCK operation in May 1941 and afterwards helped sink the U-boat supply ship BELCHEN. In September 1941 she reinforced Force H for an operation to take 9 ships to Malta, of which only one was lost. She took part in Russian convoys but returned south for the Malta convoy- Operation Harpoon- in June 1942. In August 1942 she took part in the Malta convoy-Operation Pedestal. She was torpedoed and her bow was blown off, and later was damaged by a bomb, but was able to continue in defence of the convoy. She returned to UK where repairs took until March 1943, and then joined the Eastern Fleet, bombarding Sabang (Sumatra) and supporting the landings in Burma. In 1946 she joined the American and West Indies Station. She took part in the Korean War 1950-51, and finally paid off in September1958. In this late view her she is seen with no X turret and her AA armament upgraded. She was broken up in October 1962.   (PRNM)

HMS MAURITIUS (1948)

MAURITIUS was built by Swan Hunter and completed on 1 January 1941. She served in the Atlantic and Indian Oceans, escorting convoys and carrying out patrols. In May 1943 she transferred to the Mediterranean for the Sicilian landings. It was not until that invasion in July 1943 that she first fired her guns in anger. She also took part in the Reggio and Salerno landings in September 1943. She then operated in the Bay of Biscay, before returning to the Mediterranean for the landings at Anzio. She was at the Normandy landings and turned out to be the only ship to be at Sicily, Salerno, Anzio and Normandy and carried out a total of 250 bombardments. In August 1944 she carried out anti-shipping patrols in the Bay of Biscay, severely damaging two enemy convoys. In January 1945 she was damaged in an action with 3 enemy destroyers. Post war she served in the Mediterranean and East Indies. She was refitted in 1953 and placed in reserve until she was taken to Inverkeithing to be broken up in 1965.

(World Ship Photo Library)

HMS TRINIDAD (1941)

TRINIDAD was commissioned at Devonport on 3 October 1941.This view shows her after turrets, transom stern and the large hangars fitted in the bridge structure around the forefunnel. In January 1942 she was an escort to a Russian convoy which was attacked by U-boats. In March she was on another Russian Convoy, of which 14 of the 19 ships in the convoy reached harbour despite heavy attacks of all descriptions. Whilst escorting this convoy, on 29 March, TRINIDAD and the destroyers FURY and ECLIPSE encountered 3 enemy destroyers and sank one and damaged the others. In the action TRINIDAD was hit by one of her own torpedoes but she reached the Kola Inlet under her own power. After temporary repairs, she sailed for the UK on 13 May. The next day she was attacked by aircraft, and one hit set off a serious fire, and a near miss destroyed the temporary repairs to her previous damage. On fire, and flooding, she had to be abandoned and was sunk by the destroyer MATCHLESS on 15 May 1942.

HMS GAMBIA

GAMBIA was completed by Swan Hunter on 21 February 1942. She stood by the depot ship HECLA when she was mined off South Africa and in May 1942 joined the Eastern Fleet. She served with the Royal New Zealand Navy from 1943-46, operating with the Eastern Fleet, covering air strikes on Sabang and Sourabaya and took part in the bombardment of Sabang in July 1944. She joined the British Pacific Fleet and took part in operations off Okinawa. In May and August she bombarded shore targets, and fired the last round at the Japanese home islands. She was present at the Japanese surrender in Tokyo Bay. Returned to the Royal Navy October 1946, she still retained her X turret, which was removed at Devonport that year. Later she served World-wide. She was modernised in 1957 and is seen here with her new, enclosed bridge and updated AA armament. She paid off in December 1960 and was broken up in 1968.

HMS JAMAICA

JAMAICA was completed at Barrow on 29 June 1942. She took part in operations off the Norwegian coast and covered convoys to and from Russia. In November 1942 she was at the landings in N. Africa and on 9 November put out of action 2 French destroyers. During further Russian convoys she helped drive off a German pocket battleship, heavy cruisers and destroyers from a convoy in December 1942. In 1943 she carried out patrols in the Bay of Biscay before returning to Russian convoy duty. In December 1943 she helped sink the German battlecruiser SCHARNHORST, hitting the SCHARNHORST with torpedoes and gunfire. From October 1944 to June 1945 she refitted for service in the Far East. She reached the East Indies in August 1945. In 1949 she operated against terrorists in Malaya and in 1950 was in the Korean War, carrying out bombardments, ferrying troops and coming under air attack. In 1951 she returned to UK and was modernised before taking part in the Suez operation in 1956. She paid off in September 1957 and was handed over for breaking up in November 1960.

(PRNM)

HMS BERMUDA

Built on the Clyde, BERMUDA was completed on 21 August 1942, the last of the first group of the Colony Class. This wartime photograph shows her with a radar mounted forward of her bridge. She served in the Home Fleet and took part in the landings in North Africa in November 1942, carrying out bombardments and coming under heavy air attack. She carried out patrols in the Bay of Biscay, escorted convoys to Russia, patrolled northern waters and relieved Spitzbergen in 1943. After a refit in 1944-45 during which her X turret was removed, she joined the British Pacific Fleet. She sailed from Sydney on VJ-Day as part of the Task Force for the relief of Shanghai. She helped evacuate prisoners of war from Leyte. Post war she served in the Far East, South Atlantic and Mediterranean. In 1956-57 she was modernised on the lines of GAMBIA (see page 98). She was laid up in July 1962 and towed to Briton Ferry for breaking up in August 1965.

(Dave Scoble Collection)

HMS UGANDA later HMCS QUEBEC (August 1943)

Work on the next 3 of the Colony class (UGANDA, NEWFOUNDLAND and CEYLON) was suspended in 1940, and they were completed to a modified design to counter the air threat, with a quadruple 2-pounder in place of X turret. UGANDA was completed on the Tyne on 3 January 1943. She joined the Home Fleet and undertook patrols in the Bay of Biscay before escorting convoys for North Africa and the Middle East. In July 1943 she carried out bombardments during the invasion of Sicily and the next month continued bombardments in preparation for the Salerno landings in September 1943, during which she fired 816 rounds. On 13 September she was badly damaged by a glider bomb and was repaired at Gibraltar and Charleston, South Carolina. In October 1944 she was presented to the Royal Canadian Navy. She sailed to the Pacific via the UK and Suez, joining Task Force 57 off Okinawa in April 1945. She screened carriers striking at Japanese airfields and on 14 June bombarded Truk (Caroline Islands). In July she was in operations against Tokyo before sailing for Esquimalt for a refit. She then became a training ship. Renamed QUEBEC in 1952, she paid off in 1956and was broken up in 1961.   (MPL)

HMS NEWFOUNDLAND
(14 December 1944)

NEWFOUNDLAND was completed on the Tyne on 31 December 1942. She joined the Home Fleet and undertook patrols from Plymouth against enemy shipping. In April 1943 she carried out bombardments of the islands off Italy and (in July) supported the landings at Sicily. On 23 July 1943 she was torpedoed by the German submarine U-407. With her rudder destroyed, she crossed the Atlantic steering by use of her main engines, for repairs at Boston and the Clyde, which took until November 1944. She is seen here just after being repaired, by which time her aircraft hangars had been converted into offices and extra accommodation. She then joined the British Pacific Fleet, supporting operations off New Guinea and the Caroline Islands. In July she took part in bombardments north of Tokyo and in August shelled Honshu.

HMS NEWFOUNDLAND

From 1947-50 NEWFOUNDLAND was a harbour training ship at Devonport. She was then refitted with a new bridge, lattice masts and improved fire control systems (as can be seen in this photograph which shows her new AA directors mounted abreast the foremast). In 1952 she joined the East Indies Station and in 1954 and 1956 operated against terrorists in Malaya. During the Suez operation in 1956 she was in the Red Sea and engaged and sank the Egyptian frigate DOMIAT. She was sold to Peru in 1959 and renamed ALMIRANTE GRAU. In 1973 she was renamed CAPITAN QUINONES and, in 1979, was hulked and deleted from the Peruvian lists.

(Steve Bush Collection)

HMS CEYLON

CEYLON was built by Alex Stephen at Govan and completed 13 July 1943. This view shows the squarer bridge with the 6-inch director mounted higher to clear radar fitted forward of it, fitted in these later 3 ships (compare with BERMUDA- page 100). She served in home waters, patrolling the Bay of Biscay in October 1943. She then joined the Eastern Fleet, taking part in operations against Sabang and Sourabaya and bombardments of Sabang. In January 1945 she took part in the raid on Sumatra and in April 1945 was at the landings at Rangoon. She was at the surrender at Penang in August 1945. She took part in the Korean War (1950-52), firing nearly 7,000 rounds of 6-inch ammunition and steaming over 80,000 miles. In 1956 she was refitted with a new bridge, foremast and fire control systems. She took part in the Suez operations in 1956 and later served in the Far East. She was transferred to Peru in 1960 and renamed CORONEL BOLOGNESI. She was discarded in 1982 and broken up in 1985.

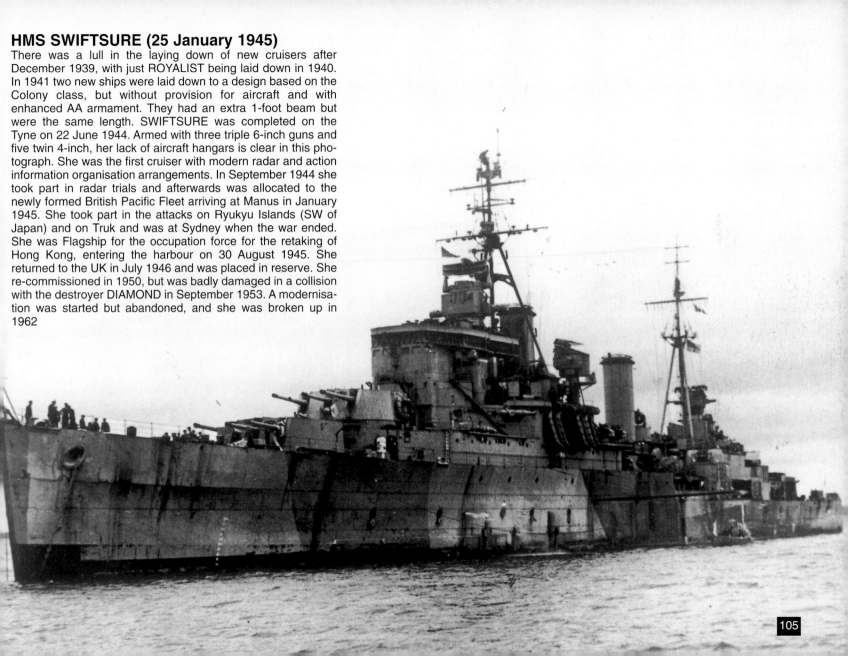

HMS SWIFTSURE (25 January 1945)

There was a lull in the laying down of new cruisers after December 1939, with just ROYALIST being laid down in 1940. In 1941 two new ships were laid down to a design based on the Colony class, but without provision for aircraft and with enhanced AA armament. They had an extra 1-foot beam but were the same length. SWIFTSURE was completed on the Tyne on 22 June 1944. Armed with three triple 6-inch guns and five twin 4-inch, her lack of aircraft hangars is clear in this photograph. She was the first cruiser with modern radar and action information organisation arrangements. In September 1944 she took part in radar trials and afterwards was allocated to the newly formed British Pacific Fleet arriving at Manus in January 1945. She took part in the attacks on Ryukyu Islands (SW of Japan) and on Truk and was at Sydney when the war ended. She was Flagship for the occupation force for the retaking of Hong Kong, entering the harbour on 30 August 1945. She returned to the UK in July 1946 and was placed in reserve. She re-commissioned in 1950, but was badly damaged in a collision with the destroyer DIAMOND in September 1953. A modernisation was started but abandoned, and she was broken up in 1962

HMCS ONTARIO (ex HMS MINOTAUR) (1955)

ONTARIO was laid down as the MINOTAUR on 20 November 1941 at Belfast, was launched on 29 July 1943 and completed on 25 May 1945, when she was presented to the Royal Canadian Navy and renamed ONTARIO (being known as 'The O Boat'). She sailed from Belfast on 26 May and headed for the Far East via Suez, arriving at Colombo on 19 August 1945, too late to take part in the war against Japan. She visited Hong Kong in October 1945 and then crossed the Pacific, arriving at Esquimalt (Canada) on 27 November 1945. She was employed as a training ship, and revisited the UK in 1953 for the Coronation Review of the Fleet at Spithead. She differed from her half sister SWIFTSURE in that she had the more modern Mk. VI directors for her 4-inch guns. The additional twin 4-inch gun in X position can be seen in this photograph. She paid off on 15 October 1958, and was broken up in Japan in 1960.

(World Ship Photo Library)

HMS SUPERB

SUPERB was not laid down until 23 June 1942, and was completed by Swan Hunter on 16 November 1945, just too late to serve in the war. Her design was similar to SWIFTSURE's, but her hull was a foot wider to improve stability, and she was fitted with Mk. VI directors for her secondary armament. Her enlarged bridge was on a superstructure with no aircraft hangar. She was Flagship of the Second Cruiser Squadron (1946-47) and then underwent a refit prior to being laid up. In 1949-50 she was again Flagship of the Second Cruiser Squadron and later served on the America and West Indies Station. She took part in the 1953 Coronation Review of the Fleet. In 1954 she was Flagship of the Home Flotillas and in 1955 was on the America and West Indies Station again. In 1957 she was in the East Indies but the next year was placed in reserve. She was never modernised and was broken up in August 1960.

HMS TIGER

As World War II neared its conclusion, priorities were re-assessed and some ships had their building suspended, whilst others were cancelled. Three cruisers of the SUPERB type, which had been laid down during the war, had work suspended in July 1946 and it was not until October 1954 that it was announced that they were to be completed to a new design. TIGER, laid down as BELLEROPHON on 1 October 1941, was completed on the Clyde on 18 March 1959. She carried two twin 6-inch guns and three twin 3-inch guns, all with high rates of fire and with individual control systems. She served in Home waters and the Mediterranean. She visited the Far East in 1962/63 and was involved in the initial operations off the Borneo/Brunei coast in December 1962. She was converted to a command helicop-ter carrier at Devonport from 1968-72 and was Flagship of FOF2 at the Jubilee Review in 1977. She paid off in April 1978 and was towed to Spain in September 1986 to be broken up.

HMS LION (17 May 1961)

LION was laid down as DEFENCE on 24 June 1942, and was launched by Scotts at Greenock on 2 September 1944. She was laid up in the Gareloch until work was resumed on her by Swan Hunter, who completed her on 20 July 1960. In this view her after twin 6-inch turret can be seen mounted level with the forecastle. These ships were much heavier than the Colony class but with basically the same hull, and so were deeper in the water and wet in a seaway. She served at home and in the Mediterranean in 1960-61. In December 1961 she carried out a cruise to South American ports and carried out exercises with the Colombian and Peruvian Navies. In 1963 she relieved her sister TIGER in the Far East and in 1963-64 served as Flagship of the Home Fleet Flotillas. In September 1964 she was at Malta for the Independence Celebrations. In 1966 to 1970 she was at Devonport for conversion to a helicopter carrier, but work was suspended and it was approved to scrap her in 1971. In 1973 she was de-equipped at Rosyth, and was broken up in 1975.

HMS BLAKE

The BLAKE had been laid down by Fairfield on 17 August 1942, and was launched on 20 December 1945. She was finally completed by Fairfield to her new design on 8 March 1961. Armed with twin 6-inch turrets forward and aft, she was a very powerfully armed ship both for surface and AA operations. In 1961 she served with the Home Fleet and in 1962 was in the Mediterranean. In July 1962 she visited the West Indies and was at Trinidad and Jamaica for Independence Celebrations. She paid off in March 1963.

HMS BLAKE

In 1965 BLAKE was taken in hand for conversion to a Command Helicopter Cruiser at Portsmouth. Her after 6-inch turret was replaced by a large hangar and flight deck, and her amidships 3-inch guns were replaced by Seacat missiles. This view and that on page 110 show the revised layout, with the forward 6-inch and 3-inch guns retained. BLAKE's conversion was completed on 23 April 1969 and she was present at the NATO Naval Review at Spithead the following month. In 1970 she undertook a World cruise. She was at Malta to cover the withdrawal from the island in 1972. She paid off in 1979, the last RN cruiser in commission, and was broken up at Cairnryan three years later.

INDEX